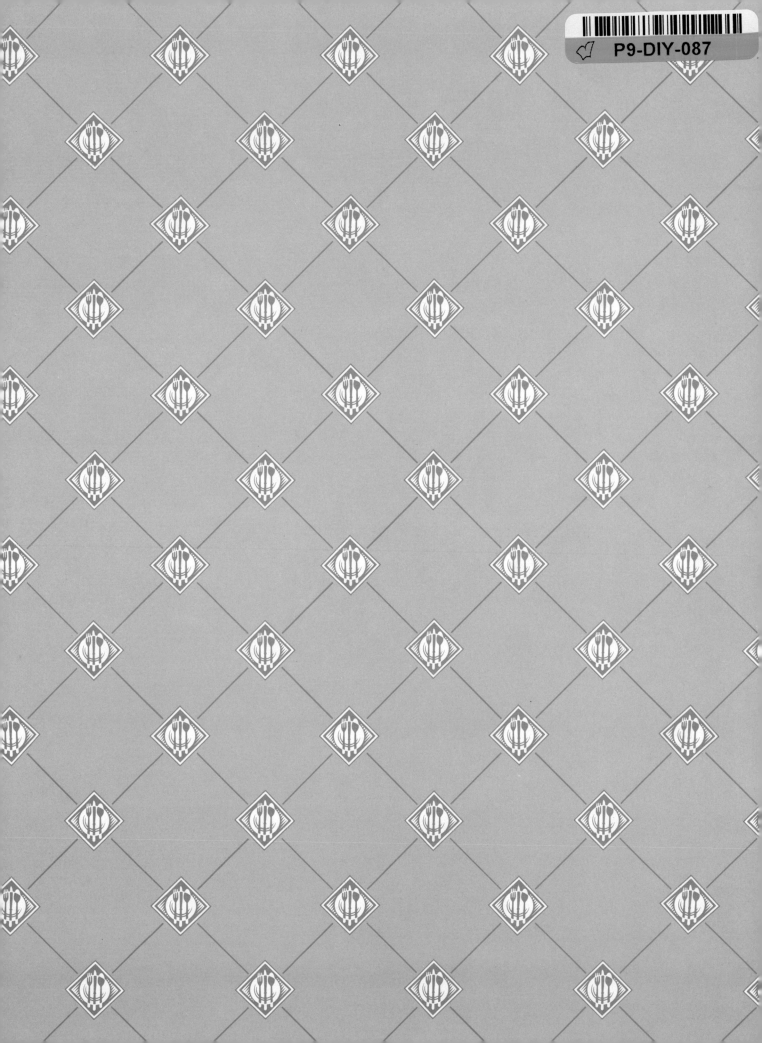

HURRY-UP
COOKIE
RECIPES

PUBLICATIONS INTERNATIONAL, LTD.

Photography on front cover and on pages 7, 13, 27, 32, 44, 49, 58, 59, 70, and 86 by Ryan Roessler Photography, Chicago.

ISBN: 1-56173-971-5

Pictured on the front cover:

1. Chocolate Chip Cordials (*page 47*)
2. Easy Peanut Butter Cookies (*page 12*)
3. Chocolate-Mint Brownies (*page 23*)
4. Chocolate Cut-Out Cookies (*page 51*)
5. Walnut Cut-Out Cookies (*page 51*)
6. Peanut Blossoms (*page 12*)
7. Decadent Brownies (*page 27*)
8. Black Forest Oatmeal Fancies (*page 55*)
9. Choco-Dipped Peanut Butter Cookies (*page 12*)
10. Double Chocolate Chip Cookies (*page 59*)
11. Marvelous Macaroons (*page 6*)
12. Heath® Bars (*page 80*)
13. Easy Apricot Oatmeal Bars (*page 71*)

Pictured on the back cover (top to bottom): Double "Topped" Brownies (*page 34*) and Original Toll House® Chocolate Chip Cookies (*page 60*).

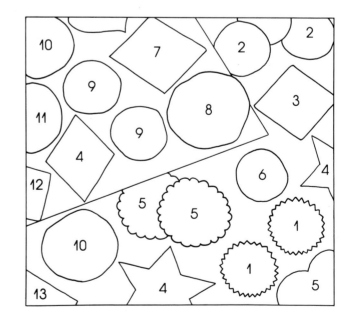

HURRY-UP
COOKIE
RECIPES

TIPS & TECHNIQUES   **4**

FAMILY CLASSICS   **6**

BUSY-DAY BROWNIES   **24**

EXTRA-SPECIAL   **40**

CHOCK FULL 'O CHIPS   **52**

QUICK-TO-FIX BARS   **66**

JUST FOR KIDS   **84**

ACKNOWLEDGMENTS   **93**

INDEX   **94**

Whether you're a newcomer to the cookie-baking scene or a real pro, these tips and techniques will help make the most of your time in the kitchen. Everything from simple drop cookies to festive cutouts will be a breeze to make simply by following these guidelines for preparing, baking and storing all kinds of cookies.

PREPARATION

The seemingly endless variety of cookies can actually be divided into five basic types: bar, drop, refrigerator, rolled and shaped. These types are determined by the consistency of the dough and how it is formed into cookies.

Bar Cookies: Always use the pan size called for in the recipe. Substituting a different pan will affect the cookies' texture. A smaller pan will give the bars a more cakelike texture and a larger pan will produce a flatter bar with a drier texture.

Most bar cookies should cool in the pan on a wire rack until barely warm before cutting. To make serving easy, remove a corner piece first; then remove the rest.

Drop Cookies: Cookies that are uniform in size and shape will finish baking at the same time. To easily shape drop cookies into a uniform size, use an ice cream scoop with a release bar. The bar usually has a number on it indicating the number of scoops that can be made from one quart of ice cream. The handiest size for

cookies is a #80 or #90 scoop. This will yield about one rounded teaspoonful of dough for each cookie.

Space mounds of dough about 2 inches apart on cookie sheets to allow for spreading unless the recipe directs otherwise.

Refrigerator Cookies: Always shape the dough into rolls before chilling. Shaping is easier if you first place the dough on a piece of waxed paper or plastic wrap. Before chilling, wrap the rolls securely in plastic wrap or air may penetrate the dough and cause it to dry out.

Use gentle pressure and a back-and-forth sawing motion when slicing the rolls so the cookies will keep their nice round shape. Rotating the roll while slicing also prevents one side from flattening.

Rolled Cookies: Chill the cookie dough before rolling for easier handling. Remove only enough dough from the refrigerator to work with at one time. Save any trimmings and reroll them all at once to prevent the dough from becoming tough.

Shaped Cookies: If the recipe calls for a specific cookie press or mold, do not try shaping the cookies by hand. The consistency of the dough was formulated to work with that specific tool.

BAKING

The best cookie sheets to use are those with little or no sides. They allow the heat to circulate easily during baking and promote even browning. Another way to promote even baking and browning is to place only one cookie sheet at a time in the center of the oven. If the cookies brown unevenly, rotate the cookie sheet from front to back halfway through the baking time. If you do use more than one sheet at a time, rotate them from top to bottom halfway through the baking time.

For best results, use shortening or a vegetable cooking spray to grease cookie sheets. Lining the cookie sheets with parchment paper is an alternative to greasing. It eliminates cleanup, bakes the cookies more evenly and allows them to cool right on the paper instead of wire racks. Allow cookie sheets to cool between batches; the dough will spread if placed on a hot cookie sheet.

Most cookies bake quickly and should be watched carefully to avoid overbaking. Check them at the minimum baking time, then watch carefully to make sure they don't burn. It is generally better to slightly underbake, rather than to overbake cookies.

Most cookies should be removed from cookie sheets immediately after baking and placed in a single layer on wire racks to cool. Fragile cookies may need to cool slightly on the cookie sheet before stacking and storing. Bar cookies and brownies may be cooled and stored in the baking pan.

STORING

Unbaked cookie dough can be refrigerated for up to one week or frozen for up to six weeks. Rolls of dough should be sealed tightly in plastic wrap; other doughs should be stored in airtight containers. Label dough with baking information for convenience.

Store soft and crisp cookies separately at room temperature to prevent changes in texture and flavor. Keep soft cookies in airtight containers. If they begin to dry out, add a piece of apple or bread to the container to help them retain moisture. Store crisp cookies in containers with loose-fitting lids to prevent moisture buildup. If they become soggy, heat undecorated cookies in a 300°F oven for 3 to 5 minutes.

Store cookies with sticky glazes, fragile decorations and icings in single layers between sheets of waxed paper. Bar cookies and brownies may be stored in their own baking pan, covered with foil or plastic wrap when cool.

As a rule, crisp cookies freeze better than soft, moist cookies. Rich, buttery bar cookies and brownies are an exception to this rule since they freeze extremely well. Freeze baked cookies in airtight containers or freezer bags for up to six months. Thaw cookies and brownies unwrapped at room temperature. Meringue-based cookies do *not* freeze well and chocolate-dipped cookies will discolor if frozen.

FAMILY CLASSICS

Marvelous Macaroons

- 1 can (8 ounces) DOLE® Crushed Pineapple in Juice
- 1 can (14 ounces) sweetened condensed milk
- 1 package (7 ounces) flaked coconut
- ½ cup margarine, melted
- ½ cup DOLE® Chopped Almonds, toasted
- 1 teaspoon grated DOLE® Lemon peel
- ¼ teaspoon almond extract
- 1 cup all-purpose flour
- 1 teaspoon baking powder

Preheat oven to 350°F. Drain pineapple well, pressing out excess juice with back of spoon. In large bowl, combine drained pineapple, milk, coconut, margarine, nuts, lemon peel and almond extract. In small bowl, combine flour and baking powder. Beat into pineapple mixture until blended. Drop heaping tablespoonfuls of dough 1 inch apart onto greased cookie sheets.

Bake 13 to 15 minutes or until lightly browned. Cool on wire racks. Garnish with whole almonds, if desired. Store in covered container in refrigerator.
Makes about 3½ dozen cookies

Chocolate Refrigerator Cookies

- 1⅔ cups all-purpose flour
- ⅓ cup NESTLE® Cocoa
- ½ teaspoon baking powder
- ½ teaspoon ground cinnamon
- ¾ cup sugar
- ½ cup (1 stick) margarine, softened
- 1 tablespoon skim milk
- 1 egg
- ¾ cup ground walnuts

In small bowl, combine flour, NESTLE® Cocoa, baking powder and cinnamon; set aside.

In large mixer bowl, beat sugar and margarine until creamy. Beat in milk and egg. Gradually beat in flour mixture. Stir in walnuts. On waxed paper, shape dough into 1½-inch diameter log; roll in waxed paper. Refrigerate 2 to 3 hours or overnight.

Preheat oven to 350°F. Cut log into ¼-inch-thick slices. Place on ungreased cookie sheets. Bake 10 minutes. Let stand on cookie sheets 2 minutes. Remove from cookie sheets; cool completely on wire racks.
Makes about 4 dozen cookies

Marvelous Macaroons

Banana Orange Softies

Cookies

1⅔ cups mashed, ripe bananas (about 3 large bananas)
¾ cup (1½ sticks) margarine or butter, softened
½ cup orange juice
2 eggs
2 teaspoons vanilla
1 teaspoon grated orange peel
2 cups QUAKER® Oats (quick or old fashioned, uncooked)
2 cups all-purpose flour
¾ teaspoon baking soda
½ teaspoon salt (optional)
¾ cup raisins

Icing

¾ cup powdered sugar
2 to 3 teaspoons orange juice
1 teaspoon grated orange peel

Preheat oven to 350°F. For Cookies, in large bowl, beat bananas, margarine and orange juice until smooth. Blend in eggs, vanilla and orange peel. Add combined dry ingredients; mix well. Stir in raisins. Drop dough by rounded tablespoonfuls onto ungreased cookie sheet. Bake 20 to 22 minutes or until light golden brown. Cool 2 minutes on cookie sheet; remove to wire rack. Cool completely.

For Icing, in small bowl, combine all ingredients; drizzle over cooled cookies. Store tightly covered.
Makes about 2½ dozen cookies

Whole Wheat Oatmeal Cookies

¾ cup BUTTER FLAVOR CRISCO®
¾ cup firmly packed brown sugar
⅓ cup apple juice
¼ cup molasses
¼ cup honey
1 egg
1 teaspoon vanilla
1 cup whole wheat flour
1 teaspoon ground cinnamon
½ teaspoon baking soda
¼ teaspoon salt
⅛ teaspoon ground nutmeg
3 cups quick oats (not instant or old fashioned), uncooked
¾ cup raisins
¾ cup chopped walnuts

1. Preheat oven to 350°F. Grease cookie sheet with BUTTER FLAVOR CRISCO®.

2. Combine BUTTER FLAVOR CRISCO®, brown sugar, juice, molasses, honey, egg and vanilla in large bowl. Beat at medium speed of electric mixer until blended.

3. Combine flour, cinnamon, baking soda, salt and nutmeg. Mix into creamed mixture at low speed until just blended. Stir in, one at a time, oats, raisins and nuts with spoon. Drop rounded tablespoonfuls of dough 2 inches apart onto cookie sheet.

4. Bake 13 to 14 minutes, or until set. Cool 5 minutes on cookie sheet. Remove to cooling rack.
Makes about 3 dozen cookies

Chocolate Oat Chewies

Chocolate Oat Chewies

- **1 package DUNCAN HINES®
  Moist Deluxe Devil's Food
  Cake Mix**
- **1⅓ cups old-fashioned oats,
  uncooked**
- **1 cup flaked coconut,
  toasted and divided**
- **¾ cup butter or margarine,
  melted**
- **2 eggs, beaten**
- **1 teaspoon vanilla extract**
- **5 bars (1.55 ounces each)
  milk chocolate, cut into
  rectangles**

1. Preheat oven to 350°F.

2. Combine cake mix, oats,
½ cup coconut, melted butter,
eggs and vanilla extract in large
bowl. Cover and refrigerate
15 minutes.

3. Shape dough into 1-inch balls.
Place balls 2 inches apart on
ungreased cookie sheet. Bake
12 minutes or until tops are
slightly cracked. Remove from
oven. Press one milk chocolate
rectangle into center of each
cookie. Sprinkle with remaining
½ cup coconut. Remove to
cooling rack.

Makes about 4½ dozen cookies

Tip: To toast coconut, spread on
cookie sheet and bake at 350°F
for 3 minutes. Stir and bake 1 to
2 minutes longer or until light
golden brown.

Honey of a Cookie

2½ cups all-purpose flour
1 cup sugar
⅔ cup LAND O LAKES® Butter,
   softened
2 eggs
¼ cup honey
2 teaspoons baking powder
½ teaspoon pumpkin pie
   spice
¼ teaspoon salt
1 teaspoon vanilla
½ cup shredded carrot
   (about 1 medium)

Preheat oven to 325°F. In large mixer bowl, combine flour, sugar, butter, eggs, honey, baking powder, pumpkin pie spice, salt and vanilla. Beat at low speed, scraping bowl often, until well mixed, 2 to 3 minutes. Stir in carrot. Shape rounded teaspoonfuls of dough into 1-inch balls. Place 2 inches apart on ungreased cookie sheets. Bake for 13 to 18 minutes, or until edges are lightly browned. Remove immediately; cool on wire racks.

Makes about 4 dozen cookies

Spiced Molasses Cookies

2¼ cups all-purpose flour
1 cup sugar
½ cup LAND O LAKES® Butter,
   softened
½ cup light molasses
¼ cup milk
1 egg
½ teaspoon baking soda
½ teaspoon ground ginger
¼ teaspoon ground cinnamon
⅛ teaspoon salt
   Sugar for rolling

In large mixer bowl, combine flour, 1 cup sugar, butter, molasses, milk, egg, baking soda, ginger, cinnamon and salt. Beat at low speed, scraping bowl often, until well mixed, 2 to 3 minutes. Cover; refrigerate until firm, at least 2 hours.

Preheat oven to 350°F. Shape rounded teaspoonfuls of dough into 1-inch balls. Roll in sugar. Place 2 inches apart on ungreased cookie sheets. Bake for 10 to 12 minutes, or until slightly firm to the touch. Remove immediately; cool on wire racks.

Makes about 4½ dozen cookies

FAMILY CLASSICS

*Top to bottom: Honey of a Cookie,
Spiced Molasses Cookies*

Easy Peanut Butter Cookies

1 (14-ounce) can EAGLE® Brand Sweetened Condensed Milk (NOT evaporated milk)
¾ to 1 cup peanut butter
1 egg
1 teaspoon vanilla extract
2 cups biscuit baking mix
   Granulated sugar

In large mixer bowl, beat sweetened condensed milk, peanut butter, egg and vanilla until smooth. Add biscuit mix; mix well. Cover; refrigerate at least 1 hour.

Preheat oven to 350°F. Shape dough into 1-inch balls. Roll in sugar. Place 2 inches apart on ungreased cookie sheets. Flatten with fork. Bake 6 to 8 minutes or until *lightly* browned. *Do not overbake.* Cool. Store tightly covered at room temperature.
   Makes about 5 dozen cookies

Choco-Dipped Peanut Butter Cookies: Shape as above; omit granulated sugar. *Do not flatten.* Bake as directed. Cool. Melt 1 pound chocolate-flavored candy coating.* Partially dip each cookie into candy coating. Place on waxed paper-lined cookie sheets. Let stand or refrigerate until firm.

Peanut Blossoms: Shape as above; *do not flatten.* Bake as directed. Press solid milk chocolate candy drop in center of each cookie immediately after baking.

*Candy coating (also called confectioners' or summer coating) is usually purchased in grocery store baking sections or in candy specialty stores.

Chocolate Almond Snowballs

1¾ cups all-purpose flour
⅔ cup NESTLE® Cocoa
2 teaspoons baking powder
¼ teaspoon salt
¾ cup granulated sugar
½ cup (1 stick) butter, melted and cooled
2 eggs
1 teaspoon almond extract
   Confectioners' sugar

Preheat oven to 350°F. In small bowl, combine flour, NESTLE® Cocoa, baking powder and salt; set aside.

In large mixer bowl, beat granulated sugar, butter, eggs and almond extract until creamy. Gradually beat in flour mixture. Roll measuring tablespoonfuls of dough into balls. Place on ungreased cookie sheets.

Bake 6 to 8 minutes. Let stand on cookie sheets 2 minutes. Remove from cookie sheets; cool completely on wire racks. Sprinkle with confectioners' sugar.
   Makes about 2½ dozen cookies

Top to bottom: Choco-Dipped Peanut Butter Cookies, Easy Peanut Butter Cookies, Peanut Blossoms

Jam-Up Oatmeal Cookies

Jam-Up Oatmeal Cookies

1 cup **BUTTER FLAVOR CRISCO**®
1½ cups firmly packed brown
       sugar
2 eggs
2 teaspoons almond extract
2 cups all-purpose flour
1 teaspoon baking powder
1 teaspoon salt
½ teaspoon baking soda
2½ cups quick oats (not instant
       or old fashioned),
       uncooked
1 cup finely chopped pecans
1 jar (12 ounces) strawberry
       jam
   Granulated sugar for
       sprinkling

1. Combine BUTTER FLAVOR CRISCO® and brown sugar in large bowl. Beat at medium speed of electric mixer until well blended. Beat in eggs and almond extract.

2. Combine flour, baking powder, salt and baking soda. Mix into creamed mixture at low speed until just blended. Stir in oats and chopped nuts with spoon. Cover. Refrigerate at least 1 hour.

3. Preheat oven to 350°F. Grease cookie sheet with BUTTER FLAVOR CRISCO®.

4. Roll out dough, half at a time, to about ¼-inch thickness on floured surface. Cut out with 2½-inch round cookie cutter. Place 1 teaspoonful jam in center of half the rounds. Top with remaining rounds. Press edges to seal. Prick centers; sprinkle with granulated sugar. Place 1 inch apart on cookie sheet.

5. Bake 12 to 15 minutes, or until lightly browned. Cool 2 minutes on cookie sheet. Remove to cooling rack.
   Makes about 2 dozen cookies

Tropical Orange Coconut Drops

2 cups sugar
1 cup LAND O LAKES® Butter, softened
3 eggs
1 teaspoon baking powder
1 teaspoon salt
1 teaspoon vanilla
1 teaspoon orange extract
3½ cups all-purpose flour
½ cup flaked coconut

Preheat oven to 350°F. In large mixer bowl, combine sugar, butter, eggs, baking powder, salt, vanilla and orange extract. Beat at low speed, scraping bowl often, until well mixed, 1 to 2 minutes. Stir in flour and coconut until well mixed, 2 to 3 minutes. Drop rounded teaspoonfuls of dough 2 inches apart onto greased cookie sheets. Bake for 8 to 12 minutes, or until edges are lightly browned. Remove immediately; cool on wire racks.

Makes about 5 dozen cookies

Blueberry Drop Cookies

1 cup fresh, canned or dry-pack frozen blueberries
¾ cup BUTTER FLAVOR CRISCO®
1 cup sugar
1½ teaspoons grated lemon peel
2 eggs
2 cups sifted all-purpose flour
2 teaspoons baking powder
¼ teaspoon salt
½ cup milk

1. Preheat oven to 375°F.

2. Rinse blueberries; spread on paper towels to dry thoroughly.

3. In large bowl, cream BUTTER FLAVOR CRISCO®, sugar and lemon peel until well blended. Add eggs, one at a time, beating well after each addition.

4. In small bowl, combine flour, baking powder and salt. Add flour mixture alternately with milk to creamed mixture, beating until smooth after each addition. Lightly fold in blueberries.

5. Drop dough by teaspoonfuls onto greased cookie sheets, 2 inches apart.

6. Bake 10 to 12 minutes, or until lightly browned. Cool on wire racks.

Makes about 5 dozen cookies

Tropical Orange Coconut Drops

Mom's Best Oatmeal Cookies

1 cup BUTTER FLAVOR CRISCO®
1½ cups firmly packed brown
    sugar
2 eggs
2 teaspoons vanilla
1½ cups all-purpose flour
1 teaspoon salt
1 teaspoon baking powder
1 teaspoon ground cinnamon
¼ teaspoon baking soda
2 cups quick oats (not instant
    or old fashioned),
    uncooked
1 cup chopped pecans
⅔ cup sesame seeds
⅔ cup flaked coconut

1. Preheat oven to 350°F.

2. Combine BUTTER FLAVOR CRISCO® and brown sugar in large bowl. Beat at medium speed of electric mixer until well blended. Beat in eggs and vanilla.

3. Combine flour, salt, baking powder, cinnamon and baking soda. Mix into creamed mixture at low speed until blended. Stir in, one at a time, oats, nuts, sesame seeds and coconut with spoon. Drop rounded tablespoonfuls of dough 2 inches apart onto ungreased cookie sheet.

4. Bake 10 minutes, or until lightly browned. Remove immediately to cooling rack.

Makes about 6 dozen cookies

Ginger Snap Oats

¾ cup BUTTER FLAVOR CRISCO®
1 cup firmly packed brown
    sugar
½ cup granulated sugar
½ cup molasses
2 teaspoons vinegar
2 eggs
1¼ cups all-purpose flour
1 tablespoon ground ginger
1½ teaspoons baking soda
½ teaspoon ground cinnamon
¼ teaspoon ground cloves
2¾ cups quick oats (not instant
    or old fashioned),
    uncooked
1½ cups raisins

1. Preheat oven to 350°F. Grease cookie sheet with BUTTER FLAVOR CRISCO®.

2. Combine BUTTER FLAVOR CRISCO®, brown sugar, granulated sugar, molasses, vinegar and eggs in large bowl. Beat at medium speed of electric mixer until well blended.

3. Combine flour, ginger, baking soda, cinnamon and cloves. Mix into creamed mixture at low speed until blended. Stir in oats and raisins with spoon. Drop rounded teaspoonfuls of dough 2 inches apart onto cookie sheet.

4. Bake 11 to 14 minutes. Cool 2 minutes on cookie sheet. Remove to cooling rack.

Makes about 5 dozen cookies

Top to bottom: Ginger Snap Oats, Mom's Best Oatmeal Cookies

Peanut Butter Jewels

3. Bake 8 to 10 minutes or until light golden brown. Cool 1 minute on cookie sheets. Remove to cooling racks. Cool completely. Store in airtight container.

Makes 3 dozen cookies

Tip: For a delicious flavor variation, try seedless red raspberry or blackberry jam.

Reese's™ *Cookies*

    2 cups all-purpose flour
    1 teaspoon baking soda
    1 cup vegetable shortening
        or ¾ cup (1½ sticks) butter
        or margarine, softened
    1 cup granulated sugar
    ½ cup firmly packed light
        brown sugar
    1 teaspoon vanilla extract
    2 eggs
    1⅔ cups (10-ounce package)
        REESE'S™ Peanut Butter
        Chips
    ⅔ cup HERSHEY'S® Semi-Sweet
        Chocolate Chips or Milk
        Chocolate Chips

Preheat oven to 350°F. In small bowl, stir together flour and baking soda. In large mixer bowl, beat shortening, granulated sugar, brown sugar and vanilla until creamy. Add eggs; beat well. Gradually add flour mixture, blending well. Stir in peanut butter chips and chocolate chips. Drop dough by rounded teaspoonfuls onto ungreased cookie sheet.

Bake 8 to 10 minutes or until lightly browned. Cool slightly; remove from cookie sheet to wire rack. Cool completely.

Makes about 5 dozen cookies

Peanut Butter Jewels

    1 package DUNCAN HINES®
        Peanut Butter Cookie Mix
    1 egg
    ¼ cup sugar
    ¼ cup cocktail peanuts, finely
        chopped
        Strawberry jam or apricot
        preserves

1. Preheat oven to 375°F.

2. Combine cookie mix, peanut butter flavor packet from mix and egg in large bowl. Stir until thoroughly blended. Shape dough into 36 (1-inch) balls. Roll half the balls in sugar and half in chopped peanuts. Place 2 inches apart on ungreased cookie sheets. Make indentation in center of each ball with finger or handle end of wooden spoon. Fill with ¼ teaspoon strawberry jam or apricot preserves.

Cocoa Snickerdoodles

1 cup butter or margarine, softened
¾ cup firmly packed brown sugar
¾ cup plus 2 tablespoons granulated sugar
2 eggs
2 cups rolled oats, uncooked
1½ cups all-purpose flour
¼ cup plus 2 tablespoons unsweetened cocoa
1 teaspoon baking soda
2 tablespoons ground cinnamon

Preheat oven to 375°F. Lightly grease cookie sheets or line with parchment paper. Beat butter, brown sugar and ¾ cup granulated sugar in large bowl until light and fluffy. Add eggs; mix well. Combine oats, flour, ¼ cup cocoa and baking soda in medium bowl. Stir into butter mixture until blended. Mix the remaining 2 tablespoons granulated sugar, cinnamon and the remaining 2 tablespoons cocoa in small bowl. Drop dough by rounded teaspoonfuls into cinnamon mixture; toss to coat. Place 2 inches apart on prepared cookie sheets.

Bake 8 to 10 minutes or until firm in center. *Do not overbake.* Remove to wire racks to cool.
Makes about 4½ dozen cookies

Banana Cookies

Prep time: 20 minutes
Chill time: 1 hour
Bake time: 20 minutes per batch

2 ripe, medium DOLE® Bananas, peeled
1½ cups all-purpose flour
½ teaspoon baking soda
½ teaspoon salt
½ teaspoon ground cinnamon
¼ teaspoon ground nutmeg
1½ cups firmly packed light brown sugar
¾ cup margarine, softened
1 egg
½ cup light dairy sour cream
1 teaspoon vanilla extract
1½ cups rolled oats, uncooked
1 cup DOLE® Golden Raisins
¾ cup DOLE® Chopped Almonds, toasted

Place bananas in blender. Process until pureed; use 1 cup for recipe. In small bowl, combine flour, baking soda, salt and spices.

In large bowl, beat brown sugar and margarine until light and fluffy. Beat in 1 cup pureed bananas, egg, sour cream and vanilla. Beat in flour mixture until well blended. Stir in oats, raisins and almonds. Cover and refrigerate dough 1 hour to firm.

Preheat oven to 350°F. Drop dough by heaping tablespoonfuls 2 inches apart onto greased cookie sheet. Bake 15 to 20 minutes or until cookies are slightly browned around edges. Cool on wire rack.
Makes about 4 dozen cookies

Lemon Cookies

1 package DUNCAN HINES®
   Lemon Supreme Cake Mix
2 eggs
⅓ cup CRISCO® Oil or
   CRISCO® PURITAN® Oil
1 tablespoon lemon juice
¾ cup chopped nuts or flaked
   coconut
   Confectioners sugar

1. Preheat oven to 375°F. Grease cookie sheet.

2. Combine cake mix, eggs, oil and lemon juice in large bowl. Beat at low speed with electric mixer until well blended. Add nuts. Shape into 1-inch balls. Place on cookie sheet, 1 inch apart.

3. Bake 6 to 7 minutes or until lightly browned. Cool 1 minute on cookie sheet. Remove to cooling rack. Dust with confectioners sugar.
   Makes about 3 dozen cookies

No-Bake Peanutty Chocolate Drops

½ cup margarine or butter
⅓ cup unsweetened cocoa
1 (14-ounce) can EAGLE®
   Brand Sweetened
   Condensed Milk (NOT
   evaporated milk)
2½ cups quick-cooking oats,
   uncooked
1 cup chopped peanuts
½ cup peanut butter

In medium saucepan over medium heat, melt margarine; stir in cocoa. Bring mixture to a boil. Remove from heat; stir in remaining ingredients. Drop dough by teaspoonfuls onto waxed paper-lined cookie sheets; refrigerate 2 hours or until set. Store loosely covered in refrigerator.
   Makes about 5 dozen cookies

Drop Sugar Cookies

2½ cups sifted all-purpose flour
¾ teaspoon salt
½ teaspoon ARM & HAMMER®
   Pure Baking Soda
½ cup butter or margarine,
   softened
½ cup vegetable shortening
1 cup sugar
1 teaspoon vanilla
1 egg
2 tablespoons milk
   Sugar

Preheat oven to 400°F. In small bowl, combine flour, salt and baking soda. In large bowl, cream butter and shortening. Gradually add sugar, beating until light and fluffy. Beat in vanilla and egg. Add dry ingredients to butter mixture; beat until smooth. Blend in milk. Drop dough by teaspoonfuls 2 inches apart onto greased cookie sheets. Flatten with bottom of greased glass that has been dipped into sugar. Bake 12 minutes or until edges are lightly browned. Cool on wire racks.
   Makes about 5½ dozen cookies

Fruit Burst Cookies

- 1 cup margarine or butter, softened
- ¼ cup sugar
- 1 teaspoon almond extract
- 2 cups all-purpose flour
- ½ teaspoon salt
- 1 cup finely chopped nuts
  SMUCKER'S® Simply Fruit

Preheat oven to 400°F. Cream margarine and sugar until light and fluffy. Blend in almond extract. Combine flour and salt; add to margarine mixture and blend well. Shape level tablespoons of dough into balls; roll in nuts. Place 2 inches apart on ungreased cookie sheets; flatten slightly. Indent centers; fill with fruit spread. Bake 10 to 12 minutes or just until lightly browned. Cool on wire racks.
Makes about 2½ dozen cookies

Oatmeal Apple Cookies

Oatmeal Apple Cookies

- ¾ cup BUTTER FLAVOR CRISCO®
- 1¼ cups firmly packed brown sugar
- 1 egg
- ¼ cup milk
- 1½ teaspoons vanilla
- 1 cup all-purpose flour
- 1¼ teaspoons ground cinnamon
- ½ teaspoon salt
- ¼ teaspoon baking soda
- ¼ teaspoon ground nutmeg
- 3 cups quick oats (not instant or old fashioned), uncooked
- 1 cup peeled, diced apples
- ¾ cup raisins (optional)
- ¾ cup coarsely chopped walnuts (optional)

1. Preheat oven to 375°F. Grease cookie sheet with BUTTER FLAVOR CRISCO®.

2. Combine BUTTER FLAVOR CRISCO®, brown sugar, egg, milk and vanilla in large bowl. Beat at medium speed of electric mixer until well blended.

3. Combine flour, cinnamon, salt, baking soda and nutmeg. Mix into creamed mixture at low speed until just blended. Stir in, one at a time, oats, apples, raisins and nuts with spoon.

4. Drop rounded tablespoonfuls of dough 2 inches apart onto cookie sheet.

5. Bake 13 minutes or until set. Cool 2 minutes on cookie sheet. Remove to cooling rack.
Makes about 2½ dozen cookies

Maple Raisin Cookies

Cookies

2¼ cups all-purpose flour
1 cup granulated sugar
¾ cup LAND O LAKES® Butter,
    softened
¾ cup applesauce
1 egg
1 teaspoon pumpkin pie
    spice
½ teaspoon baking soda
½ teaspoon salt
1 cup raisins
½ cup chopped walnuts

Frosting

4 cups powdered sugar
½ cup LAND O LAKES® Butter,
    softened
3 to 4 tablespoons milk
½ teaspoon maple extract
    Raisins

Preheat oven to 375°F. For Cookies, in large mixer bowl, combine flour, granulated sugar, butter, applesauce, egg, pumpkin pie spice, baking soda and salt. Beat at low speed, scraping bowl often, until well mixed, 2 to 3 minutes. Stir in raisins and nuts. Drop rounded teaspoonfuls of dough 2 inches apart onto greased cookie sheets. Bake for 10 to 12 minutes, or until lightly browned. Remove immediately; cool completely on wire racks.

For Frosting, in small mixer bowl, combine powdered sugar, butter, milk and maple extract. Beat at medium speed, scraping bowl often, until light and fluffy, 3 to 4 minutes. Spread over cooled cookies. Place 2 raisins in center of each cookie.
Makes about 3 dozen cookies

Maple Raisin Cookies

Spritz

1 cup BUTTER FLAVOR CRISCO®
½ cup sugar
1 egg
¾ teaspoon salt
¾ teaspoon vanilla
½ teaspoon almond extract
2¼ cups all-purpose flour

1. Preheat oven to 400°F. Combine BUTTER FLAVOR CRISCO® and sugar in large bowl. Beat at medium speed of electric mixer until well blended. Beat in egg, salt, vanilla and almond extract. Stir in flour.

2. Place dough in cookie press. Press into desired shapes 2 inches apart on ungreased cookie sheet.

3. Bake 5 to 7 minutes or until set, but not brown. Cool 1 minute. Remove to wire rack; cool completely.
Makes about 4 dozen cookies

Note: Tint dough with a few drops of food color, or ice and decorate if desired.

Cranberry Orange Ricotta Cheese Brownies

Filling

1 cup ricotta cheese
¼ cup sugar
3 tablespoons whole-berry cranberry sauce
2 tablespoons cornstarch
1 egg
¼ to ½ teaspoon grated orange peel
4 drops red food color (optional)

Brownies

½ cup (1 stick) butter or margarine, melted
¾ cup sugar
1 teaspoon vanilla extract
2 eggs
¾ cup all-purpose flour
½ cup HERSHEY'S® Cocoa
½ teaspoon baking powder
½ teaspoon salt

Preheat oven to 350°F. Grease 9-inch square baking pan. For Filling, in small mixer bowl, beat ricotta cheese, sugar, cranberry sauce, cornstarch and egg until smooth. Stir in orange peel and food color, if desired.

For Brownies, in small bowl, stir together butter, sugar and vanilla; add eggs, beating well. Stir together flour, cocoa, baking powder and salt; add to butter mixture, mixing thoroughly. Spread half of chocolate batter in prepared pan. Spread cheese mixture over top. Drop remaining chocolate batter by teaspoonfuls onto cheese mixture. Bake 40 to 45 minutes or until wooden toothpick inserted in center comes out clean. Cool completely on wire rack. Cut into squares. Refrigerate leftovers.

Makes about 16 brownies

Cranberry Orange Ricotta Cheese Brownies

Blonde Brickle Brownies

White Chocolate Brownies

**1 package DUNCAN HINES®
   Brownies Plus Milk
   Chocolate Chunks Mix**
2 eggs
⅓ cup water
**⅓ cup CRISCO® Oil or
   CRISCO® PURITAN® Oil**
**¾ cup coarsely chopped
   white chocolate**
¼ cup sliced natural almonds

1. Preheat oven to 350°F. Grease bottom of 13×9×2-inch pan.

2. Combine brownie mix, eggs, water and oil in large bowl. Stir with spoon until well blended, about 50 strokes. Stir in white chocolate. Spread in pan. Sprinkle top with almonds. Bake 25 to 28 minutes or until set. Cool completely on wire rack. Cut into bars.

*Makes 4 dozen small or
2 dozen large brownies*

Blonde Brickle Brownies

1⅓ cups flour
½ teaspoon baking powder
¼ teaspoon salt
2 eggs
½ cup granulated sugar
**½ cup firmly packed brown
   sugar**
**⅓ cup butter or margarine,
   melted**
1 teaspoon vanilla extract
¼ teaspoon almond extract
**1 package (6 ounces) HEATH®
   BITS 'O BRICKLE®, divided**
**½ cup chopped pecans
   (optional)**

Preheat oven to 350°F. Grease 8-inch square pan. Mix flour with baking powder and salt; set aside. In large bowl, beat eggs well. Gradually beat in granulated sugar and brown sugar until thick and creamy. Add melted butter, vanilla and almond extract; mix well. Gently stir in flour mixture until moistened. Fold in ⅔ cup BITS 'O BRICKLE® and nuts. Pour into prepared pan.

Bake 30 minutes. Remove from oven; immediately sprinkle remaining BITS 'O BRICKLE® over top. Cool completely in pan on wire rack. Cut into squares.

Makes about 16 brownies

Decadent Brownies

½ cup dark corn syrup
½ cup butter or margarine
6 squares (1 ounce each)
   semi-sweet chocolate
¾ cup sugar
3 eggs
1 cup all-purpose flour
1 cup chopped walnuts
1 teaspoon vanilla
   Fudge Glaze (recipe
   follows)

Preheat oven to 350°F. Grease 8-inch square pan. Combine corn syrup, butter and chocolate in large heavy saucepan. Place over low heat; stir until chocolate is melted and ingredients are blended. Remove from heat; blend in sugar. Stir in eggs, flour, chopped walnuts and vanilla. Spread batter evenly in prepared pan. Bake 20 to 25 minutes or just until center is set. *Do not overbake.* Meanwhile prepare Fudge Glaze. Remove brownies from oven. Spread glaze immediately over hot brownies. Cool in pan on wire rack. Cut into 2-inch squares. Garnish with chopped nuts, if desired.   ***Makes 16 brownies***

Fudge Glaze

3 squares (1 ounce each)
   semi-sweet chocolate
2 tablespoons dark corn
   syrup
1 tablespoon butter or
   margarine
1 teaspoon light cream or
   milk

Combine chocolate, corn syrup and butter in small heavy saucepan. Stir over low heat until chocolate is melted; mix in cream.

German Chocolate Brownies

1 package DUNCAN HINES®
   Brownies Plus Milk
   Chocolate Chunks Mix
½ cup firmly packed brown
   sugar
2 tablespoons butter or
   margarine, softened
1 tablespoon all-purpose
   flour
½ cup chopped pecans
½ cup flaked coconut

1. Preheat oven to 350°F. Grease bottom of 13×9×2-inch pan.

2. Prepare brownies following package directions. Spread in pan.

3. Combine brown sugar, butter and flour in small bowl. Mix until well blended. Stir in pecans and coconut. Sprinkle mixture over batter. Bake 25 to 30 minutes or until topping is browned. Cool completely on wire rack. Cut into bars.

   Makes about 2 dozen brownies

Decadent Brownies

Quick No-Bake Brownies

1 cup finely chopped nuts
2 (1-ounce) squares unsweetened chocolate
1 (14-ounce) can EAGLE® Brand Sweetened Condensed Milk (NOT evaporated milk)
2 to 2½ cups vanilla wafer crumbs (about 48 to 60 wafers)

In buttered 9-inch square pan, sprinkle ¼ cup nuts. In heavy saucepan, over low heat, melt chocolate with sweetened condensed milk. Cook and stir until mixture thickens, about 10 minutes. Remove from heat; stir in crumbs and ½ cup nuts. Spread evenly into prepared pan. Top with remaining ¼ cup nuts. Chill 4 hours or until firm. Cut into squares. Store loosely covered at room temperature.
Makes about 2 dozen brownies

Chocolate-Mint Brownies

½ cup butter or margarine
2 squares (1 ounce each) unsweetened chocolate
2 eggs
1 cup firmly packed light brown sugar
½ cup all-purpose flour
1 teaspoon vanilla
Mint Frosting (recipe follows)
Chocolate Glaze (recipe follows)

Preheat oven to 350°F. Grease and flour 8-inch square pan. Melt butter and chocolate in small heavy saucepan over low heat; stir to blend. Remove from heat; cool. Beat eggs in medium bowl until light. Add brown sugar, beating well. Blend in chocolate mixture. Stir in flour and vanilla. Spread batter evenly in prepared pan. Bake 30 minutes or until firm in center. Cool in pan on wire rack. Prepare Mint Frosting. Spread over top; refrigerate until firm. Prepare Chocolate Glaze. Drizzle over frosting; refrigerate until firm. Cut into 2-inch squares.   *Makes 16 brownies*

Mint Frosting

1½ cups powdered sugar
2 to 3 tablespoons light cream or milk
1 tablespoon butter or margarine, softened
½ teaspoon peppermint extract
1 to 2 drops green food coloring

Blend powdered sugar, 2 tablespoons cream and butter in small bowl until smooth. Add more cream, if necessary, to make frosting of spreading consistency. Blend in peppermint extract and enough green food coloring to make a pale mint-green color.

Chocolate Glaze

½ cup semi-sweet chocolate chips
2 tablespoons butter or margarine

Place chocolate chips and butter in small bowl over hot water. Stir until melted and smooth.

Fancy Walnut Brownies

1. Preheat oven to 350°F. Place 24 (2-inch) foil cupcake liners on baking sheets.

2. For Brownies, combine brownie mix, egg, water and oil in large bowl. Stir with spoon until well blended, about 50 strokes. Stir in contents of walnut packet from mix. Fill each cupcake liner with 2 generous tablespoons batter. Bake 20 to 25 minutes or until set. Cool completely. Remove cupcake liners. Turn brownies upside down on cooling rack.

3. For Glaze, combine confectioners sugar and milk or water. Blend until smooth. Spoon glaze over first brownie to completely cover. Top immediately with walnut half. Repeat for remaining brownies. (Allow glaze to set before adding Chocolate Drizzle.)

4. For Chocolate Drizzle, place chocolate chips and shortening in reclosable sandwich bag; seal. Place bag in hot water for several minutes. Dry with paper towel. Knead until blended and chocolate is smooth. Snip off pinpoint corner of bag. Drizzle chocolate over brownies.

Makes 2 dozen brownies

Tip: Place waxed paper under cooling rack to catch excess glaze and drizzle.

Fancy Walnut Brownies

Brownies

1 package DUNCAN HINES® Brownies Plus Walnuts Mix
1 egg
⅓ cup water
⅓ cup CRISCO® Oil or CRISCO® PURITAN® Oil

Glaze

4½ cups confectioners sugar
½ cup milk or water
24 walnut halves, for garnish

Chocolate Drizzle

⅓ cup semi-sweet chocolate chips
1 tablespoon CRISCO® Shortening

Rocky Road Brownies

½ cup butter or margarine
½ cup unsweetened cocoa
1 cup sugar
1 egg
½ cup all-purpose flour
¼ cup buttermilk
1 teaspoon vanilla
1 cup miniature
   marshmallows
1 cup coarsely chopped
   walnuts
1 cup (6 ounces) semi-sweet
   chocolate chips

Preheat oven to 350°F. Lightly grease 8-inch square pan. Combine butter and cocoa in medium-sized heavy saucepan over low heat, stirring constantly until smooth. Remove from heat; stir in sugar, egg, flour, buttermilk and vanilla. Mix until smooth. Spread batter evenly in prepared pan.

Bake 25 minutes or until center feels dry. (*Do not overbake or brownies will be dry.*) Remove from oven; sprinkle marshmallows, walnuts and chocolate chips over top. Return to oven for 3 to 5 minutes or just until topping is warmed enough to hold together. Cool in pan on wire rack. Cut into 2-inch squares.   **Makes 16 brownies**

Irish Coffee Brownies

One 11½-ounce package
   (2 cups) NESTLE®
   Toll House® Milk
   Chocolate Morsels,
   divided
½ cup (1 stick) butter
½ cup sugar
2 eggs
1 teaspoon vanilla extract
2 tablespoons Irish whiskey
2 teaspoons NESCAFE®
   Classic Instant Coffee
1 cup all-purpose flour

Preheat oven to 350°F. In small saucepan over low heat, combine 1 cup NESTLE® Toll House® Milk Chocolate Morsels and butter; stir until morsels are melted and mixture is smooth. Cool to room temperature. In large bowl, combine sugar and eggs; beat until thick and lemon colored. Gradually beat in chocolate mixture and vanilla extract. In cup, combine Irish whiskey and NESCAFE® Classic Instant Coffee; stir until dissolved. Add to chocolate mixture. Gradually blend in flour. Pour into foil-lined 8-inch square baking pan.

Bake 25 to 30 minutes. Immediately sprinkle remaining 1 cup NESTLE® Toll House® Milk Chocolate Morsels on top. Let stand until morsels are shiny and soft; spread evenly. Cool completely on wire rack; cut into 2-inch squares.

Makes 16 brownies

Rocky Road Brownies

Peanut Butter Chip Brownies

Peanut Butter Chip Brownies

½ cup butter or margarine
4 squares (1 ounce each)
    semi-sweet chocolate
½ cup sugar
2 eggs
1 teaspoon vanilla
½ cup all-purpose flour
1 package (12 ounces)
    peanut butter chips
1 cup (6 ounces) milk
    chocolate chips

Preheat oven to 350°F. Butter 8-inch square pan. Melt butter and semi-sweet chocolate in small heavy saucepan over low heat, stirring just until chocolate melts completely. Remove from heat; cool. Beat sugar and eggs in large bowl until light. Blend in vanilla and chocolate mixture. Stir in flour until blended; fold in peanut butter chips. Spread batter evenly in prepared pan.

Bake 25 to 30 minutes or just until firm and dry in center. Remove from oven; sprinkle milk chocolate chips over top. Place pan on wire rack. When chocolate chips have melted, spread over brownies. Refrigerate until chocolate topping is set. Cut into 2-inch squares.   *Makes 16 brownies*

Butterscotch Brownies

2 cups all-purpose flour
2 teaspoons baking powder
½ teaspoon salt
½ cup (1 stick) butter
One 12-ounce package (2 cups) NESTLE® Toll House® Butterscotch Flavored Morsels
1 cup firmly packed brown sugar
4 eggs
1 teaspoon vanilla extract
1 cup chopped nuts

Preheat oven to 350°F. Grease 15½×10½×1-inch baking pan. In small bowl, combine flour, baking powder and salt; set aside.

In small saucepan, over low heat, melt butter. Remove from heat. Stir in butterscotch morsels until morsels are melted and mixture is smooth. Transfer to large mixer bowl. Stir in brown sugar; cool 5 minutes. Beat in eggs and vanilla extract. Blend in flour mixture. Stir in nuts. Spread in pan.

Bake 20 to 25 minutes. Cool completely on wire rack. Cut into bars.

Makes about 35 brownies

Bittersweet Brownies

MAZOLA® No Stick cooking spray
4 squares (1 ounce each) unsweetened chocolate, melted
1 cup sugar
½ cup HELLMANN'S® or BEST FOODS® Real, Light or Cholesterol Free Reduced Calorie Mayonnaise
2 eggs
1 teaspoon vanilla
¾ cup flour
½ teaspoon baking powder
¼ teaspoon salt
½ cup chopped walnuts

Preheat oven to 350°F. Spray 8×8×2-inch baking pan with cooking spray. In large bowl, combine chocolate, sugar, mayonnaise, eggs and vanilla until smooth. Stir in flour, baking powder and salt until well blended. Stir in walnuts. Spread evenly in prepared pan.

Bake 25 to 30 minutes or until wooden toothpick inserted Into center comes out clean. Cool in pan on wire rack. Cut into 2-inch squares. *Makes 16 brownies*

Double "Topped" Brownies

Brownies

1 package DUNCAN HINES® Brownies Plus Double Fudge Mix
2 eggs
⅓ cup water
¼ cup CRISCO® Oil or CRISCO® PURITAN® Oil
½ cup flaked coconut
½ cup chopped nuts

Frosting

3 cups confectioners sugar
⅓ cup butter or margarine, softened
1½ teaspoons vanilla extract
2 to 3 tablespoons milk

Topping

3 squares (1 ounce each) unsweetened chocolate
1 tablespoon butter or margarine

Double "Topped" Brownies

1. Preheat oven to 350°F. Grease bottom of 13×9×2-inch pan.

2. For Brownies, combine brownie mix, fudge packet from mix, eggs, water and oil in large bowl. Stir with spoon until well blended, about 50 strokes. Stir in coconut and nuts. Spread in pan. Bake 27 to 30 minutes or until set. Cool completely on wire rack.

3. For Frosting, combine confectioners sugar, ⅓ cup butter and vanilla extract. Stir in milk, 1 tablespoon at a time, until frosting is of spreading consistency. Spread over brownies. Refrigerate until frosting is firm, about 30 minutes.

4. For Topping, melt chocolate and 1 tablespoon butter in small bowl over hot water; stir until smooth. Drizzle over frosting. Refrigerate until chocolate is firm, about 15 minutes. Cut into bars.

Makes about 48 brownies

Tip: Chocolate topping can be prepared in microwave oven. Place chocolate and butter in microwave-safe bowl and microwave at MEDIUM (50% power) for 2 to 2½ minutes; stir until smooth.

All American Heath® Brownies

⅓ cup butter or margarine
1 ounce (1 square)
    unsweetened chocolate
1 cup sugar
2 eggs
1 teaspoon vanilla
1 cup flour
½ teaspoon baking powder
¼ teaspoon salt
1 package (6 ounces)
    HEATH® Bits

Preheat oven to 350°F. Grease bottom only of 8-inch square baking pan.

In 1½-quart saucepan over low heat, melt butter and chocolate, stirring several times. Blend in sugar. Add eggs, one at a time, beating after each addition. Blend in vanilla. In small bowl, mix together flour, baking powder and salt; add to chocolate mixture and blend. Spread batter in pan.

Bake 20 minutes. Remove from oven; sprinkle with Heath® Bits. Cover tightly with foil and cool completely on wire rack. Cut into bars.

Makes about 1 dozen brownies

All American Heath® Brownies

Ultimate Brownies

Prep time: 10 minutes
Bake time: 35 minutes

½ cup MIRACLE WHIP® Salad
    Dressing
2 eggs
¼ cup cold water
1 package (20 to 23 ounces)
    fudge brownie mix
3 bars (7 ounces each) milk
    chocolate, divided

• Preheat oven to 350°F.

• In large bowl, mix salad dressing, eggs and water until well blended. Stir in brownie mix, mixing just until moistened.

• Coarsely chop 2 chocolate bars; stir into brownie mixture. Pour into greased 13×9-inch baking pan. Chop remaining chocolate bar; set aside.

• Bake 30 to 35 minutes or until edges begin to pull away from sides of pan. Immediately top with remaining chocolate bar, chopped. Let stand about 5 minutes or until melted; spread evenly over brownies. Cool.

Makes about 2 dozen brownies

Brownie Pizza

1 package DUNCAN HINES®
    Brownies Plus Milk
    Chocolate Chunks Mix
1 egg
⅓ cup CRISCO® Oil or
    CRISCO® PURITAN® Oil
2 tablespoons water
    Strawberry slices
    Kiwi wedges
    Pineapple chunks
    Apricot halves
    Vanilla ice cream
    Chocolate syrup

1. Preheat oven to 350°F. Grease 13-inch round pizza pan.

2. Combine brownie mix, egg, oil and water in large bowl. Stir with spoon until well blended, about 50 strokes. Spread in pan. Bake 23 to 27 minutes. Cool completely on wire rack.

3. Decorate with assorted fruit and cut into wedges. Top with scoops of ice cream, then drizzle with chocolate syrup.
    Makes about 12 servings

Best Brownies

½ cup (1 stick) butter or
    margarine, melted
1 cup sugar
1 teaspoon vanilla extract
2 eggs
½ cup all-purpose flour
⅓ cup HERSHEY'S® Cocoa
¼ teaspoon baking powder
¼ teaspoon salt
½ cup chopped nuts
    (optional)
    Creamy Brownie Frosting
    (recipe follows)

Preheat oven to 350°F. Grease 9-inch square baking pan. In medium bowl, stir together melted butter, sugar and vanilla. Add eggs; beat well with spoon. In small bowl, stir together flour, cocoa, baking powder and salt; gradually add to egg mixture, beating until well blended. Stir in nuts, if desired. Spread batter evenly in prepared pan.

Bake 20 to 25 minutes or until brownies begin to pull away from sides of pan. Cool completely on wire rack. Frost with Creamy Brownie Frosting. Cut into squares.
    Makes about 16 brownies

Creamy Brownie Frosting

3 tablespoons butter or
    margarine, softened
3 tablespoons HERSHEY'S®
    Cocoa
1 tablespoon light corn syrup
    or honey
½ teaspoon vanilla extract
1 cup powdered sugar
1 to 2 tablespoons milk

In small mixer bowl, beat butter, cocoa, corn syrup and vanilla until blended. Add powdered sugar and milk; beat until frosting is of spreading consistency.
    Makes about 1 cup frosting

Brownie Pizza

Raspberry Fudge Brownies

Preheat oven to 350°F. Butter and flour 8-inch square pan. Melt butter and bittersweet chocolate in small heavy saucepan over low heat. Remove from heat; cool. Beat eggs, sugar and vanilla in large bowl until light. Beat in chocolate mixture. Stir in flour, baking powder and salt until just blended. Spread ¾ of batter in prepared pan; sprinkle almonds over top.

Bake 10 minutes. Remove from oven; spread preserves over almonds. Carefully spoon remaining batter over preserves, smoothing top. Bake 25 to 30 minutes or just until top feels firm.

Remove from oven; sprinkle chocolate chips over top. Let stand a few minutes until chips melt, then spread evenly over brownies.

Cool completely in pan on wire rack. When chocolate is set, cut into 2-inch squares.

Makes 16 brownies

Raspberry Fudge Brownies

½ cup butter or margarine
3 squares (1 ounce each) bittersweet chocolate*
2 eggs
1 cup sugar
1 teaspoon vanilla
¾ cup all-purpose flour
¼ teaspoon baking powder
    Dash salt
½ cup sliced or slivered almonds
½ cup raspberry preserves
1 cup milk chocolate chips

*Bittersweet chocolate is available in specialty food stores. One square unsweetened chocolate plus 2 squares semi-sweet chocolate may be substituted.

Apple Sauce Brownies

1 cup firmly packed brown
    sugar
½ cup margarine or butter,
    softened
2 eggs
1 cup MOTT'S® Regular or
    Cinnamon Apple Sauce
1 teaspoon vanilla
1 cup all-purpose flour
¼ cup unsweetened cocoa
1 teaspoon ground cinnamon
½ teaspoon baking powder
½ teaspoon baking soda
¼ teaspoon salt
½ cup chopped nuts
    Powdered sugar
    Unsweetened cocoa
¼ teaspoon ground cinnamon

Preheat oven to 350°F. Grease
9-inch square pan. In large
bowl, combine brown sugar,
margarine and eggs; mix well.
Stir in apple sauce and vanilla;
blend thoroughly. Stir in flour,
¼ cup cocoa, 1 teaspoon
cinnamon, baking powder,
baking soda and salt; mix well.
Stir in nuts.

Bake 25 to 35 minutes or until
wooden toothpick inserted in
center comes out clean. Cool in
pan on wire rack. Just before
serving, use foil strips to make
striped design with powdered
sugar, cocoa and ¼ teaspoon
cinnamon. Cut into bars.
Makes about 16 brownies

Supreme Chocolate Saucepan Brownies

1 cup (2 sticks) butter or
    margarine
2 cups sugar
½ cup HERSHEY'S® Cocoa
4 eggs, beaten
⅔ cup all-purpose flour
½ teaspoon salt
¼ teaspoon baking soda
2 teaspoons vanilla extract
2 cups (12-ounce package)
    HERSHEY'S® Semi-Sweet
    Chocolate Chips *or*
    1¾ cups (10-ounce
    package) HERSHEY'S®
    Semi-Sweet Chocolate
    Chunks
½ cup macadamia nuts,
    coarsely chopped

Preheat oven to 350°F. Grease
13×9×2-inch baking pan. In
medium saucepan over low
heat, melt butter. Add sugar
and cocoa; stir to blend.
Remove from heat. Stir in eggs.
In small bowl, stir together flour,
salt and baking soda; stir into
chocolate mixture. Stir in vanilla,
chocolate chips and nuts.
Spread into prepared pan.
Bake 30 to 35 minutes or until
brownies begin to crack slightly
and pull away from sides of
pan. *Do not overbake.* Cool
completely on wire rack; cut
into bars.
Makes about 2 dozen brownies

EXTRA-SPECIAL

Greeting Card Cookies

½ cup (1 stick) butter or
   margarine, softened
¾ cup sugar
1 egg
1 teaspoon vanilla extract
1½ cups all-purpose flour
⅓ cup HERSHEY'S® Cocoa
½ teaspoon baking powder
½ teaspoon baking soda
¼ teaspoon salt
   Decorative Frosting
   (recipe follows)

In large mixer bowl, beat butter, sugar, egg and vanilla until light and fluffy. In small bowl, stir together flour, cocoa, baking powder, baking soda and salt; add to butter mixture, blending well. Refrigerate about 1 hour or until firm enough to roll. Cut 2½×4-inch cardboard rectangle for pattern; wrap in plastic wrap.

Preheat oven to 350°F. On lightly floured board or between two pieces of waxed paper, roll out half of dough to ¼-inch-thickness. Place pattern on dough; cut through dough around pattern with sharp paring knife. (Save dough trimmings and reroll for remaining cookies.) Carefully place cutouts on lightly greased cookie sheet. Bake 8 to 10 minutes or until set. Cool 1 minute on cookie sheet. (If cookies have lost their shape, trim irregular edges while cookies are still hot.) Carefully transfer to cooling rack. Repeat procedure with remaining dough. Prepare Decorative Frosting; spoon into pastry bag fitted with decorating tip. Pipe names or greetings onto cooled cookies; decorate as desired.
   Makes about 1 dozen cookies

Decorative Frosting: In small mixer bowl, combine 3 cups powdered sugar and ⅓ cup shortening; gradually add 2 to 3 tablespoons milk, beating until smooth and slightly thickened. Divide frosting; tint with food coloring, if desired. Cover until ready to use.

Greeting Card Cookies

Raspberry-Filled Chocolate Ravioli

Raspberry-Filled Chocolate Ravioli

  2 squares (1 ounce each)
      bittersweet or semi sweet
      chocolate
  1 cup butter or margarine,
      softened
  ½ cup granulated sugar
  1 egg
  1 teaspoon vanilla
  ½ teaspoon chocolate extract
  ¼ teaspoon baking soda
      Dash salt
  2½ cups all-purpose flour
  1 to 1¼ cups seedless
      raspberry jam
      Powdered sugar

Melt chocolate in top of double boiler over hot, not boiling, water. Remove from heat; cool. Cream butter and granulated sugar in large bowl until blended. Add egg, vanilla, chocolate extract, baking soda, salt and melted chocolate; beat until light. Blen d in flour to make a stiff dough. Divide dough in half. Cover; refrigerate until firm.

Preheat oven to 350°F. Lightly grease cookie sheets or line with parchment paper. Roll out dough, half at a time, 1/8 inch thick between 2 sheets of plastic wrap. Remove top sheet of plastic. (If dough gets too soft and sticks to plastic, refrigerate until firm.) Cut dough into 1½-inch squares. Place half of the squares 2 inches apart on prepared cookie sheets. Place about 1/2 teaspoon jam in center of each square; top with another square. Using fork, press edges of squares together to seal, then pierce center of each square. Bake 10 minutes or just until edges are browned. Remove to wire racks to cool. Dust lightly with powdered sugar.

Makes about 6 dozen cookies

Chocolate-Dipped Brandy Snaps

½ cup (1 stick) butter
½ cup sugar
⅓ cup dark corn syrup
½ teaspoon ground
    cinnamon
¼ teaspoon ground ginger
1 cup all-purpose flour
2 teaspoons brandy
One 6-ounce package (1 cup)
    NESTLE® Toll House®
    Semi-Sweet
    Chocolate Morsels
1 tablespoon vegetable
    shortening
⅓ cup finely chopped nuts

Preheat oven to 300°F. In heavy gauge saucepan, combine butter, sugar, dark corn syrup, cinnamon and ginger; cook over medium heat, stirring constantly, until melted and smooth. Remove from heat; stir in flour and brandy. Drop dough by rounded teaspoonfuls 3 inches apart onto ungreased cookie sheets. (Do *not* bake more than 6 cookies at one time.) Bake 10 to 12 minutes. Remove from oven; let stand a few seconds. Remove from cookie sheets and immediately roll around wooden spoon handle to form a cylinder; cool completely.

Combine over hot (not boiling) water, NESTLE® Toll House® Semi-Sweet Chocolate Morsels and vegetable shortening; stir until morsels are melted and mixture is smooth. Dip each Brandy Snap halfway in melted chocolate. Sprinkle with nuts; set on waxed paper-lined cookie sheets. Refrigerate until set. Store in airtight container in refrigerator.
Makes about 3 dozen cookies

Jack O'Lantern Cookies

1 cup butter or margarine,
    softened
½ cup firmly packed light
    brown sugar
½ cup granulated sugar
2 eggs
1 teaspoon vanilla extract
1⅓ cups all-purpose flour
1 teaspoon baking soda
1½ cups rolled oats (quick or
    old-fashioned), uncooked
1 package (6 ounces) dried
    fruit bits
1½ cups (6 ounces)
    Gjetost cheese, cut
    into ¼-inch cubes
1 cup chopped walnuts
2 cups confectioners' sugar
2 to 3 tablespoons milk
    Orange and green
    food coloring

Preheat oven to 375°F. In small bowl with electric mixer, cream butter and sugars until light and fluffy. Blend in eggs and vanilla. In another small bowl, combine flour and baking soda; stir into dough. Blend in oats, fruit, cheese and walnuts. Shape tablespoons of dough into balls and place 2 inches apart on ungreased cookie sheets. Press down lightly with glass. Bake 10 minutes or until golden. Cool on wire racks.

In medium bowl, blend confectioners' sugar with enough milk to make a thick frosting. Divide in half. Color one-half with green food coloring and the remainder with orange food coloring. Decorate cookies in pumpkin design.
Makes about 4½ dozen cookies

Favorite recipe from **Norseland Foods**

Little Raisin Logs

1 cup butter or margarine, softened
⅓ cup sugar
2 teaspoons brandy (optional)
2 teaspoons vanilla
½ teaspoon salt
2 cups all-purpose flour
1 cup SUN-MAID® Raisins, finely chopped
1 cup DIAMOND® Walnuts, finely chopped
1 package (6 ounces) real semi-sweet chocolate pieces
3 tablespoons vegetable shortening

Preheat oven to 350°F. In large bowl, cream butter and sugar. Beat in brandy, vanilla and salt. Stir in flour, raisins and walnuts. Pinch off dough and roll with hands on lightly floured board into logs about ½ inch in diameter and 2½ inches long.

Bake on ungreased cookie sheet 15 to 20 minutes. *Cookies do not brown.* Remove to wire rack to cool.

Meanwhile, in top of double boiler, melt chocolate and shortening over simmering water, blending thoroughly. When cookies have cooled, dip one end into melted chocolate. Place on wire rack to set.
Makes about 6 dozen cookies

Almond Cream Cheese Cookies

3 ounces cream cheese, softened
1 cup butter, softened
1 cup sugar
1 egg yolk
1 tablespoon milk
⅛ teaspoon almond extract
2½ cups sifted cake flour
1 cup BLUE DIAMOND® Sliced Natural Almonds, toasted

Beat cream cheese with butter and sugar until fluffy. Blend in egg yolk, milk and almond extract. Gradually mix in cake flour. Gently stir in almonds. (Dough will be sticky.) Divide dough in half; place each half on large sheet of waxed paper. Working through waxed paper, shape each half into 12×1½-inch roll. Refrigerate until very firm.

Preheat oven to 325°F. Cut rolls into ¼-inch-thick slices. Bake on ungreased cookie sheets 10 to 15 minutes or until edges are golden. *Cookies should not brown.* Cool on wire racks.
Makes about 4 dozen cookies

Top to bottom: Almond Cream Cheese Cookies, Little Raisin Logs

EXTRA-SPECIAL

Half-Hearted Valentine Cookies

Cookies

¾ cup sugar
1 cup LAND O LAKES® Butter, softened
1 package (3 ounces) cream cheese, softened
1 egg
1 teaspoon peppermint extract
3 cups all-purpose flour

Glaze

1 cup semi-sweet real chocolate chips
¼ cup LAND O LAKES® Butter

For Cookies, in large mixer bowl, combine all cookie ingredients except flour. Beat at medium speed, scraping bowl often, until light and fluffy. Add flour; beat until mixed. Divide dough into halves. Wrap in waxed paper. Refrigerate until firm, at least 2 hours.

Preheat oven to 375°F. Roll out dough on lightly floured surface to ¼-inch thickness. Cut out with floured heart-shaped cutters. Place 1 inch apart on ungreased cookie sheets. Bake for 7 to 10 minutes, or until edges are very lightly browned. Remove immediately; cool completely on wire racks.

For Glaze, in small saucepan, melt chocolate chips and butter, stirring occasionally, over low heat until melted, 4 to 6 minutes. Dip half of each heart into chocolate. Refrigerate on waxed paper-lined cookie sheets until firm. Store, covered, in refrigerator.

Makes about 3½ dozen cookies

Chocolate Rum Balls

½ cup butter or margarine, softened
⅓ cup granulated sugar
1 egg yolk
1 tablespoon dark rum
1 teaspoon vanilla
1 cup all-purpose flour
¼ cup unsweetened cocoa
1 cup finely chopped walnuts or pecans
Powdered sugar

Cream butter, granulated sugar and egg yolk in large bowl until light and fluffy. Blend in rum and vanilla. Stir in flour, cocoa and nuts; mix well. Cover; refrigerate until firm, about 1 hour.

Preheat oven to 350°F. Lightly grease cookie sheets or line with parchment paper. Shape dough into 1-inch balls. Place 2 inches apart on prepared cookie sheets. Bake 15 to 20 minutes or until firm. Remove to wire racks to cool. Roll in powdered sugar.

Makes about 3 dozen cookies

Half-Hearted Valentine Cookies

46

Chocolate Chip Cordials

Cookies

1 package DUNCAN HINES®
    Chocolate Chip
    Cookie Mix
1 egg
2 teaspoons water
1 cup chopped pecans
¼ cup chopped red candied
    cherries
¼ cup flaked coconut
    Pecan halves, for garnish
    Red or green candied
        cherry halves, for garnish

Chocolate Glaze

1 square (1 ounce)
    semi-sweet chocolate
1½ tablespoons butter or
    margarine

1. Preheat oven to 375°F.
Place 1¾-inch paper liners in
28 mini muffin cups.

2. For Cookies, combine cookie
mix, buttery flavor packet from
mix, egg and water in large
bowl. Stir until well blended. Stir
in chopped pecans, chopped
cherries and coconut. Fill cups
with dough. Top with pecan or
cherry half. Bake 13 to 15 minutes
or until light golden brown. Cool
completely on wire rack.

3. For Chocolate Glaze, melt
chocolate and butter in small
bowl over hot water. Stir until
smooth. Drizzle over cordials.
Refrigerate until chocolate is
firm. Store in airtight container.

Makes 28 cordials

Tip: To microwave glaze, place
chocolate and butter in
microwave-safe bowl.
Microwave at MEDIUM
(50% power) for 45 to 60
seconds; stir until smooth.

Chocolate Chip Cordials

Spicy Pumpkin Cookies

2 cups BUTTER FLAVOR
    CRISCO®
2 cups sugar
1 can (16 ounces) pumpkin
2 eggs
2 teaspoons vanilla
4 cups sifted flour
2 teaspoons baking powder
2 teaspoons ground
    cinnamon
1 teaspoon salt
1 teaspoon baking soda
1 teaspoon ground nutmeg
½ teaspoon ground allspice
2 cups raisins
1 cup chopped nuts

Preheat oven to 350°F. In large
mixing bowl, cream BUTTER
FLAVOR CRISCO® and sugar.
Add pumpkin, eggs and
vanilla; beat well. Combine
flour, baking powder, cinnamon,
salt, baking soda, nutmeg and
allspice. Add to dough; mix well.
Stir in raisins and nuts. Drop
dough by rounded teaspoonfuls
2 inches apart onto greased
cookie sheet. Bake 12 to 15
minutes. Cool on wire rack. If
desired, frost with your favorite
vanilla frosting.

Makes about 7 dozen cookies

Austrian Tea Cookies

1½ cups sugar, divided
½ cup butter, softened
½ cup vegetable shortening
1 egg, beaten
½ teaspoon vanilla extract
2 cups all-purpose flour
2 cups HONEY ALMOND
    DELIGHT® Brand Cereal,
    crushed to 1 cup
½ teaspoon baking powder
¼ teaspoon ground cinnamon
14 ounces almond paste
2 egg whites
5 tablespoons raspberry or
    apricot jam, warmed

In large bowl, beat 1 cup sugar, butter and shortening. Add egg and vanilla; mix well. Stir in flour, cereal, baking powder and cinnamon until well blended. Refrigerate 1 to 2 hours or until firm.

Preheat oven to 350°F. Roll dough out on lightly floured surface to ¼-inch thickness; cut into 2-inch circles with floured cookie cutter. Place on ungreased cookie sheet; set aside. In small bowl, beat almond paste, egg whites and remaining ½ cup sugar until smooth. With pastry tube fitted with medium-sized star tip, pipe almond paste mixture ½ inch thick on top of each cookie along outside edge. Place ¼ teaspoon jam in center of each cookie, spreading out to paste. Bake 8 to 10 minutes or until lightly browned. Let stand 1 minute before removing from cookie sheet. Cool on wire rack.
Makes about 3½ dozen cookies

Almond Fudge Cups

Pastry
¾ cup butter or margarine,
    softened
⅓ cup sugar
2 cups all-purpose flour
1 tablespoon almond- or
    fruit-flavored liqueur
    or water
1 teaspoon vanilla

Filling
1 cup (6 ounces) semi-sweet
    chocolate chips
¾ cup blanched almonds
2 eggs
½ cup sugar
    Dash salt

For Pastry, preheat oven to 350°F. Lightly grease 3 dozen miniature (1¾-inch) muffin pan cups or small tart shells. Cream butter and sugar in large bowl until blended. Add flour, liqueur and vanilla; stir to make moist crumbs. Divide crumbs evenly among muffin cups; press to cover bottoms and sides of cups completely.

For Filling, place chocolate chips and almonds in food processor or blender. Process until finely ground. Beat eggs in medium bowl until thick; stir in sugar and salt. Blend in chocolate mixture. Spoon filling into unbaked pastry shells. Bake 20 minutes or until filling is set. Cool in pans on wire racks. Store in airtight containers.
Makes 3 dozen cookies

Austrian Tea Cookies

Chocolate Biscotti

1½ cups all-purpose flour
½ cup NESTLE® Cocoa
1½ teaspoons baking powder
½ teaspoon baking soda
⅔ cup sugar
3 tablespoons butter, softened
2 eggs
½ teaspoon almond extract
½ cup almonds, coarsely chopped

Preheat oven to 350°F. In small bowl, combine flour, NESTLE® Cocoa, baking powder and baking soda; set aside.

In large mixer bowl, beat sugar, butter, eggs and almond extract until creamy. Gradually beat in flour mixture. Stir in almonds. Divide dough in half. On greased cookie sheet, shape into two 12-inch-long logs.

Bake 25 minutes. Place cookie sheet on wire rack; cool 5 minutes. Cut log into ½-inch-thick slices; return slices to cookie sheet, cut sides down. Bake 20 minutes longer. Cool completely on wire rack.
Makes about 4 dozen cookies

Ice Cream Cookie Sandwiches

Ice Cream Cookies

2 squares (1 ounce each) unsweetened chocolate
1 cup butter, softened
1 cup powdered sugar
4 egg yolks
1 teaspoon vanilla
3 cups all-purpose flour
Powdered sugar

Melt chocolate in top of double boiler over hot, not boiling, water. Remove from heat; cool. Cream butter and 1 cup powdered sugar in large bowl until blended. Add egg yolks, vanilla and melted chocolate; beat until light. Blend in flour to make stiff dough. Divide into 4 parts. Shape each part into a roll, 1½ inches in diameter. Wrap in plastic wrap; refrigerate until firm, at least 30 minutes or up to 2 weeks. (Or freeze up to 6 weeks.)

Preheat oven to 350°F. Line cookie sheets with parchment paper or leave ungreased. Cut rolls into ⅛-inch-thick slices; place 2 inches apart on ungreased cookie sheets. Bake 8 to 10 minutes or just until set, but not browned. Remove to wire racks to cool. Dust with powdered sugar.
Makes about 8 dozen cookies

Ice Cream Cookie Sandwiches:
Prepare and bake cookies as directed; cool completely. Spread softened ice cream on bottoms of half the cookies. Top with remaining cookies, bottom sides down. Dust tops with powdered sugar; serve immediately.
Makes about 4 dozen sandwich cookies

Chocolate Cherry Cookies

2 squares (1 ounce each) unsweetened chocolate
½ cup butter or margarine, softened
½ cup sugar
1 egg
2 cups cake flour
1 teaspoon vanilla
¼ teaspoon salt
Maraschino cherries, well drained (about 48)
1 cup (6 ounces) semi sweet or milk chocolate chips

Melt unsweetened chocolate in top of double boiler over hot, not boiling, water. Remove from heat; cool. Cream butter and sugar in large bowl until light. Add egg and melted chocolate; beat until fluffy. Stir in cake flour, vanilla and salt until well ble nded. Cover; refrigerate until firm, about 1 hour.

Preheat oven to 400°F. Lightly grease cookie sheets or line with parchment paper. Shape dough into 1-inch balls. Place 2 inches apart on prepared cookie sheets. With knuckle of a finger, make a deep indentation in center of each ball. Place a cherry into each indentation. Bake 8 minutes or just until set. Meanwhile, melt chocolate chips in small bowl over hot water. Stir until melted. Remove cookies to wire racks. Drizzle melted chocolate over tops while still warm. Refrigerate until chocolate is set.

Makes about 4 dozen cookies

Walnut Cut-Out Cookies

3½ cups unsifted flour
1 tablespoon baking powder
½ teaspoon salt
1 (14-ounce) can EAGLE® Brand Sweetened Condensed Milk (NOT evaporated milk)
¾ cup margarine or butter, softened
2 eggs
1 tablespoon vanilla extract
1½ cups finely chopped walnuts

In small bowl, combine flour, baking powder and salt. In large mixer bowl, beat sweetened condensed milk, margarine, eggs and vanilla until well blended. Add dry ingredients and walnuts; mix well. Refrigerate 2 hours.

Preheat oven to 350°F. On floured surface, knead dough to form a smooth ball. Divide into thirds. On well-floured surface, roll out each portion to ⅛-inch thickness. Cut out with floured cookie cutter. Reroll as necessary to use all dough. Place cookies 1 inch apart on greased cookie sheets. Bake 10 to 12 minutes or until lightly browned around edges. *Do not overbake.* Cool on wire racks. Frost and decorate as desired. Store loosely covered at room temperature.

Makes about 7 dozen cookies

Chocolate Cut-Out Cookies: Decrease flour to 3 cups. Combine ½ cup unsweetened cocoa with dry ingredients. Proceed as directed.

Makes about 7 dozen cookies

CHOCK FULL O' CHIPS

Ivory Chip Strawberry Fudge Drops

⅔ cup BUTTER FLAVOR CRISCO®
1 cup sugar
1 egg
½ teaspoon strawberry extract
   or flavor
½ cup buttermilk*
6 tablespoons pureed frozen
   sweetened strawberries
1¾ cups all-purpose flour
6 tablespoons unsweetened
   cocoa powder
¾ teaspoon baking soda
½ teaspoon salt
1½ cups white baking chips

1. Preheat oven to 350°F. Grease cookie sheet with BUTTER FLAVOR CRISCO®.

2. Combine BUTTER FLAVOR CRISCO®, sugar, egg and strawberry extract in large bowl. Beat at medium speed of electric mixer until well blended. Beat in buttermilk and strawberry puree.

3. Combine flour, cocoa, baking soda and salt. Mix into creamed mixture at low speed of electric mixer until blended. Stir in white baking chips with spoon.

4. Drop rounded tablespoonfuls of dough 2 inches apart onto cookie sheet.

5. Bake 11 to 12 minutes, or until tops spring back when pressed lightly. Remove immediately to cooling rack.

Makes about 2½ dozen cookies

*You may substitute 1½ teaspoons lemon juice or vinegar plus enough milk to make ½ cup for the buttermilk. Stir. Wait 5 minutes before using.

Ivory Chip Strawberry Fudge Drops

Whole Grain Chippers

- 1 cup butter or margarine, softened
- 1 cup firmly packed light brown sugar
- ⅔ cup granulated sugar
- 2 eggs
- 1 teaspoon baking soda
- 1 teaspoon vanilla
  Pinch salt
- 1 cup whole wheat flour
- 1 cup all-purpose flour
- 2 cups uncooked rolled oats
- 1 package (12 ounces) semi-sweet chocolate chips
- 1 cup sunflower seeds

Preheat oven to 375°F. Lightly grease cookie sheets or line with parchment paper. Cream butter with sugars and eggs in large bowl until light and fluffy. Beat in baking soda, vanilla and salt. Blend in flours and oats to make a stiff dough. Stir in chocolate chips. Shape rounded teaspoonfuls of dough into balls; roll in sunflower seeds. Place 2 inches apart on prepared cookie sheets. Bake 8 to 10 minutes or until firm. *Do not overbake.* Cool a few minutes on cookie sheets, then remove to wire racks to cool completely.

Makes about 6 dozen cookies

San Francisco Cookies

Prep time: 15 minutes
Bake time: 16 minutes per batch

- 2 extra-ripe, medium DOLE® Bananas, peeled and cut into chunks
- 2 cups granola
- 1½ cups all-purpose flour
- 1 cup firmly packed brown sugar
- 1 teaspoon baking powder
- 1 teaspoon ground cinnamon
- 2 eggs
- ½ cup margarine, melted
- ¼ cup vegetable oil
- 1 cup (6 ounces) chocolate chips

Preheat oven to 350°F. In food processor or blender container, process bananas until pureed (1 cup). Combine granola, flour, sugar, baking powder and cinnamon in large mixing bowl. Beat in pureed bananas, eggs, margarine and oil. Fold in chocolate chips.

Drop dough by ¼ cupfuls onto greased cookie sheets. Spread dough into 2½- to 3-inch circles. Bake 16 minutes. Remove to wire racks to cool.

Makes about 16 cookies

Black Forest Oatmeal Fancies

- 1 cup BUTTER FLAVOR CRISCO®
- 1 cup firmly packed brown sugar
- 1 cup granulated sugar
- 2 eggs
- 2 teaspoons vanilla
- 1⅔ cups all-purpose flour
- 1 teaspoon baking soda
- 1 teaspoon salt
- ½ teaspoon baking powder
- 3 cups quick oats (not instant or old fashioned), uncooked
- 1 package white baking bars (6 ounces), coarsely chopped
- 3 baking bars (2 ounces each) semi-sweet chocolate, coarsely chopped
- ½ cup coarsely chopped red candied cherries
- ½ cup sliced almonds

1. Preheat oven to 375°F.

2. Combine BUTTER FLAVOR CRISCO®, brown sugar, granulated sugar, eggs and vanilla in large bowl. Beat at medium speed of electric mixer until well blended.

3. Combine flour, baking soda, salt and baking powder. Mix into creamed mixture at low speed until well blended. Stir in, one at a time, oats, white baking bars, semi-sweet chocolate, cherries and nuts with spoon.

4. Drop rounded tablespoonfuls of dough 2 inches apart onto ungreased cookie sheet.

5. Bake 9 to 11 minutes, or until set. Cool 2 minutes on cookie sheet. Remove to cooling rack.

Makes about 3 dozen cookies

Black Forest Oatmeal Fancies

Oatmeal Scotchies

1¼ cups all-purpose flour
1 teaspoon baking soda
½ teaspoon salt
½ teaspoon ground
   cinnamon
1 cup (2 sticks) butter,
   softened
¾ cup granulated sugar
¾ cup firmly packed brown
   sugar
2 eggs
1 teaspoon vanilla extract
   or grated rind of 1
   orange
3 cups quick or
   old-fashioned oats,
   uncooked
One 12-ounce package
   (2 cups) NESTLE®
   Toll House® Butterscotch
   Flavored Morsels

Preheat oven to 375°F. In small bowl, combine flour, baking soda, salt and cinnamon; set aside.

In large mixer bowl, beat butter, granulated sugar, brown sugar, eggs and vanilla extract until creamy. Gradually beat in flour mixture. Stir in oats and NESTLE® Toll House® Butterscotch Flavored Morsels. Drop dough by measuring tablespoonfuls onto ungreased cookie sheets.

Bake 7 to 8 minutes for chewy cookies or 9 to 10 minutes for crisp cookies. Let stand on cookie sheets 2 minutes. Remove from cookie sheets; cool completely on wire racks.
Makes about 4 dozen cookies

Oatmeal Scotchie Pan Cookies:
Preheat oven to 375°F. Spread dough in greased 15½×10½×1-inch baking pan. Bake 18 to 22 minutes or until very lightly browned. Cool completely on wire rack. Cut into bars.
Makes about 35 bars

Chocolate Peanut Butter Chip Cookies

8 (1-ounce) squares
   semi-sweet chocolate
3 tablespoons margarine
   or butter
1 (14-ounce) can EAGLE®
   Brand Sweetened
   Condensed Milk (NOT
   evaporated milk)
2 cups biscuit baking mix
1 teaspoon vanilla extract
1 cup peanut butter-flavored
   chips

Preheat oven to 350°F. In large saucepan over low heat, melt chocolate and margarine with sweetened condensed milk; remove from heat. Add biscuit mix and vanilla; beat at low speed of electric mixer until smooth and well blended. Cool to room temperature. Stir in chips. Shape dough into 1¼-inch balls. Place 2 inches apart on ungreased cookie sheets.

Bake 6 to 8 minutes or until tops are slightly crusted. *Do not overbake.* Cool. Store tightly covered at room temperature.
Makes about 4 dozen cookies

Oatmeal Scotchies

Left to right: Double Chocolate Chip Cookies, Forgotten Chips Cookies

Forgotten Chips Cookies

  2 egg whites
  ⅛ teaspoon cream of tartar
  ⅛ teaspoon salt
  ⅔ cup sugar
  1 teaspoon vanilla extract
  1 cup HERSHEY'S® Semi-Sweet
     Chocolate Chips or Milk
     Chocolate Chips

Preheat oven to 375°F. Lightly grease cookie sheet. In small mixer bowl, beat egg whites with cream of tartar and salt until soft peaks form. Gradually add sugar, beating until stiff peaks form. Carefully fold in vanilla extract and chocolate chips. Drop mixture by teaspoonfuls onto prepared cookie sheet. Place cookie sheet in preheated oven; immediately turn off oven and allow cookies to remain in oven six hours or overnight without opening door. Remove cookies from cookie sheet. Store in airtight container in cool, dry place.

Makes about 2½ dozen cookies

Double Chocolate Chip Cookies

2 cups all-purpose flour
1 teaspoon baking soda
½ teaspoon salt
4 cups (24-ounce package) HERSHEY'S® Semi-Sweet Chocolate Chips, divided
¾ cup (1½ sticks) butter or margarine, softened
¾ cup sugar
2 eggs

Preheat oven to 350°F. In small bowl, stir together flour, baking soda and salt. In medium microwave-safe bowl, place 2 cups chocolate chips. Microwave at HIGH (100%) 1½ minutes; stir. Microwave at HIGH an additional 30 seconds or until chips are melted and smooth when stirred; cool slightly. In large mixer bowl, beat butter and sugar until light and fluffy. Add eggs; beat well. Blend in melted chocolate. Gradually add flour mixture, beating well. Stir in remaining 2 cups chips. Drop dough by rounded teaspoonfuls onto ungreased cookie sheet.

Bake 8 to 9 minutes. *Do not overbake*. Cookies should be soft. Cool slightly; remove from cookie sheet to wire rack. Cool completely.
   Makes about 5 dozen cookies

Easy Peanutty Snickerdoodles

2 tablespoons sugar
2 teaspoons ground cinnamon
1 package (15 ounces) golden sugar cookie mix
1 egg
1 tablespoon water
1 cup REESE'S® Peanut Butter Chips

Preheat oven to 375°F. In small bowl, stir together sugar and cinnamon; set aside. In medium bowl, combine cookie mix (and enclosed flavor packet), egg and water; mix with spoon or fork until thoroughly blended. Stir in peanut butter chips. Shape dough into 1-inch balls. (If dough is too soft, cover and refrigerate about 1 hour.) Roll balls in reserved cinnamon-sugar mixture; place on ungreased cookie sheet.

Bake 8 to 10 minutes or until very lightly browned. Cool slightly; remove from cookie sheet to wire rack. Cool completely.
   Makes about 2 dozen cookies

Easy Peanutty Snickerdoodles

Original Toll House® Chocolate Chip Cookies

2¼ cups all-purpose flour
1 teaspoon baking soda
1 teaspoon salt
1 cup (2 sticks) butter, softened
¾ cup granulated sugar
¾ cup firmly packed brown sugar
1 teaspoon vanilla extract
2 eggs
One 12-ounce package (2 cups) NESTLE® Toll House® Semi-Sweet Chocolate Morsels
1 cup chopped nuts

Preheat oven to 375°F. In small bowl, combine flour, baking soda and salt; set aside.

In large mixer bowl, beat butter, granulated sugar, brown sugar and vanilla extract until creamy. Beat in eggs. Gradually beat in flour mixture. Stir in NESTLE® Toll House® Semi-Sweet Chocolate Morsels and nuts. Drop dough by rounded measuring tablespoonfuls onto ungreased cookie sheets.

Bake 9 to 11 minutes or until edges are golden brown. Let stand on cookie sheets 2 minutes. Remove from cookie sheets; cool completely on wire racks.

Makes about 5 dozen cookies

Toll House® Pan Cookies: Preheat oven to 375°F. Spread dough in greased 15½×10½×1-inch baking pan. Bake 20 to 25 minutes. Cool completely on wire rack. Cut into 2-inch bars.

Makes about 35 bars

Heavenly Almond Treats

1 cup BUTTER FLAVOR CRISCO®
⅔ cup firmly packed dark brown sugar
½ cup granulated sugar
1 egg, beaten
¼ cup sweetened condensed milk
1 teaspoon vanilla
1 teaspoon almond extract
2 cups all-purpose flour
1 teaspoon baking soda
1 teaspoon salt
2 cups flaked coconut
2 cups milk chocolate chips
1 cup slivered almonds

1. Preheat oven to 375°F.

2. Combine BUTTER FLAVOR CRISCO®, brown sugar and granulated sugar in large bowl. Beat at medium speed of electric mixer until well blended.

3. Combine egg, milk, vanilla and almond extract. Mix into creamed mixture at low speed until blended.

4. Combine flour, baking soda and salt. Mix into creamed mixture at low speed until just blended. Stir in, one at a time, coconut, chocolate chips and nuts with spoon.

5. Drop rounded tablespoonfuls of dough 2 inches apart onto ungreased cookie sheet. Form dough into 3×1-inch ovals.

6. Bake 12 minutes, or until golden brown. Cool 3 minutes on cookie sheet. Remove to cooling rack.

Makes about 4 dozen cookies

Original Toll House®
Chocolate Chip Cookies

Chocolate Chip Oatmeal
Raisin Cookies

Chocolate Chip Oatmeal Raisin Cookies

1 package DUNCAN HINES®
    Oatmeal Raisin
    Cookie Mix
1 egg
1 tablespoon water
½ cup chopped walnuts
½ cup semi-sweet chocolate
    chips
2 tablespoons sugar
¾ teaspoon ground cinnamon

1. Preheat oven to 375°F.

2. Combine cookie mix, buttery flavor packet from mix, egg and water in large bowl. Stir until thoroughly blended. Stir in walnuts and chocolate chips. Shape dough into 1-inch balls. Place balls 2 inches apart on ungreased cookie sheet.

3. Combine sugar and cinnamon in small bowl. Flatten cookies with greased glass dipped in cinnamon-sugar mixture. Bake 8 to 10 minutes or until lightly browned. Cool 1 minute on cookie sheet. Remove to cooling rack.
    Makes about 3 dozen cookies

Ultimate Chocolate Chip Cookies

¾ cup BUTTER FLAVOR CRISCO®
1¼ cups firmly packed brown
    sugar
2 tablespoons milk
1 tablespoon vanilla
1 egg
1¾ cups all-purpose flour
1 teaspoon salt
¾ teaspoon baking soda
1 cup semi-sweet chocolate
    chips
1 cup coarsely chopped
    pecans*

1. Preheat oven to 375°F.

2. Combine BUTTER FLAVOR CRISCO®, brown sugar, milk and vanilla in large bowl. Beat at medium speed of electric mixer until well blended. Beat in egg.

3. Combine flour, salt and baking soda. Mix into creamed mixture at low speed until just blended. Stir in chocolate chips and nuts with spoon.

4. Drop rounded tablespoonfuls of dough 3 inches apart onto ungreased cookie sheet.

5. Bake 8 to 10 minutes for chewy cookies (they will look light and moist). *Do not overbake.* Bake 11 to 13 minutes for crisp cookies. Cool 2 minutes on cookie sheet. Remove to cooling rack.
    Makes about 3 dozen cookies

*You may substitute an additional ½ cup semi-sweet chocolate chips for the pecans.

Variations:

Drizzle: Combine 1 teaspoon BUTTER FLAVOR CRISCO® and 1 cup semi-sweet chocolate .

chips or 1 cup white melting chocolate, cut into small pieces, in microwave-safe measuring cup. Microwave at MEDIUM (50%) for 1 minute; stir. Repeat until smooth (or melt on rangetop in small saucepan on very low heat). To thin, add a little more BUTTER FLAVOR CRISCO®. Drizzle back and forth over cooled cookies. Sprinkle with nuts before chocolate hardens, if desired. To harden chocolate quickly, place cookies in refrigerator for a few minutes.

Chocolate Dipped: Melt chocolate as directed for Drizzle. Dip one end of cooled cookie halfway up in chocolate. Sprinkle with finely chopped nuts before chocolate hardens. Place on waxed paper until chocolate is firm. To harden chocolate quickly, place cookies in refrigerator for a few minutes.

Hershey's® Vanilla Chip Chocolate Cookies

Hershey's® Vanilla Chip Chocolate Cookies

1¼ cups (2½ sticks) butter or margarine, softened
2 cups sugar
2 eggs
2 teaspoons vanilla extract
2 cups all-purpose flour
¾ cup HERSHEY'S® Cocoa
1 teaspoon baking soda
½ teaspoon salt
1⅔ cups (10-ounce package) HERSHEY'S® Vanilla Milk Chips

Preheat oven to 350°F. In large mixer bowl, beat butter and sugar until creamy. Add eggs and vanilla extract; beat until light and fluffy. Stir together flour, cocoa, baking soda and salt; gradually blend into butter mixture. Stir in vanilla milk chips. Drop dough by rounded teaspoonfuls onto ungreased cookie sheet.

Bake 8 to 9 minutes. *Do not overbake.* Cookies should be soft. They will puff while baking and flatten upon cooling. Cool slightly; remove from cookie sheet to wire rack. Cool completely.
  Makes about 4½ dozen cookies

Peanut Butter Sunshine Cookies

½ cup BUTTER FLAVOR CRISCO®
¾ cup JIF® Extra Crunchy
  Peanut Butter
1 cup sugar
½ cup orange marmalade
2 eggs
1 teaspoon vanilla
2 cups all-purpose flour
1 tablespoon baking powder
½ teaspoon salt
1 cup butterscotch-flavored
  chips

1. Preheat oven to 350°F. Grease cookie sheet with BUTTER FLAVOR CRISCO®.

2. Combine BUTTER FLAVOR CRISCO®, JIF® Extra Crunchy Peanut Butter and sugar in large bowl. Beat at medium speed of electric mixer until well blended. Beat in marmalade, eggs and vanilla.

3. Combine flour, baking powder and salt. Mix into creamed mixture at low speed until just blended. Stir in butterscotch chips with spoon.

4. Drop rounded teaspoonfuls of dough 2 inches apart onto cookie sheet.

5. Bake 10 to 12 minutes or until lightly browned. Cool 2 minutes on cookie sheet. Remove to cooling rack.
   Makes about 4 dozen cookies

Hershey's® More Chips Chocolate Chip Cookies

1½ cups (3 sticks) butter,
  softened
1 cup granulated sugar
1 cup firmly packed light
  brown sugar
3 eggs
2 teaspoons vanilla extract
3⅓ cups all-purpose flour
1½ teaspoons baking soda
¾ teaspoon salt
4 cups (24-ounce package)
  HERSHEY'S® Semi-Sweet
  Chocolate Chips

Preheat oven to 375°F. In large mixer bowl, beat butter, granulated sugar and brown sugar until creamy. Add eggs and vanilla; beat until light and fluffy. In small bowl, stir together flour, baking soda and salt; gradually beat into butter mixture. Stir in chocolate chips. Drop dough by rounded teaspoonfuls onto ungreased cookie sheet.

Bake 8 to 10 minutes or until lightly browned. Cool slightly; remove from cookie sheet to wire rack. Cool completely.
Makes about 7½ dozen cookies

Double Nut Chocolate Chip Cookies

Double Nut Chocolate Chip Cookies

**1 package DUNCAN HINES®
    Yellow Cake Mix**
**½ cup butter or margarine,
    melted**
1 egg
**1 cup semi-sweet chocolate
    chips**
½ cup finely chopped pecans
**1 cup sliced almonds,
    divided**

1. Preheat oven to 375°F. Grease cookie sheet.

2. Combine cake mix, butter and egg in large bowl. Mix at low speed with electric mixer until just blended. Stir in chocolate chips, pecans and ¼ cup sliced almonds. Shape rounded tablespoonfuls of dough into balls. Place remaining ¾ cup sliced almonds in shallow bowl. Press top of each cookie into almonds. Place on cookie sheet, 1 inch apart.

3. Bake 9 to 11 minutes or until lightly browned. Cool 2 minutes on cookie sheet. Remove to cooling rack.
    Makes 3 to 3½ dozen cookies

Toffee-Bran Bars

¾ cup all-purpose flour
¾ cup NABISCO® 100% Bran, divided
1¼ cups firmly packed light brown sugar, divided
½ cup BLUE BONNET® Margarine, melted
2 eggs, slightly beaten
1 teaspoon DAVIS® Baking Powder
1 teaspoon vanilla extract
1 cup semi-sweet chocolate chips
½ cup flaked coconut, toasted
⅓ cup chopped walnuts

Preheat oven to 350°F. In small bowl, combine flour, ½ cup bran, ½ cup brown sugar and margarine. Press in bottom of 13×9×2-inch baking pan. Bake 10 minutes; set aside.

In medium bowl, with electric mixer at high speed, beat remaining ¼ cup bran, ¾ cup brown sugar, eggs, baking powder and vanilla until thick and foamy. Spread over prepared crust. Bake an additional 25 minutes or until set. Remove pan from oven. Sprinkle with chocolate chips; let stand for 5 minutes. Spread softened chocolate evenly over baked layer. Immediately sprinkle coconut and walnuts in alternating diagonal strips over chocolate. Cool completely in pan on wire rack. Cut into 3×1½-inch bars. Store in airtight container.

Makes 2 dozen bars

Toffee-Bran Bars, Chewy Bar Cookies (page 68)

Chewy Bar Cookies

- ½ cup BLUE BONNET® Margarine, softened
- 1 cup firmly packed light brown sugar
- 2 eggs
- 3 (1¼-ounce) packages Mix 'n Eat CREAM OF WHEAT® Cereal, Apple 'n Cinnamon Flavor
- ⅔ cup all-purpose flour
- 2 teaspoons baking powder
- 1 cup finely chopped walnuts

Preheat oven to 350°F. In large bowl, with electric mixer at medium speed, beat margarine and brown sugar until creamy. Beat in eggs until light and fluffy. Stir in cereal, flour and baking powder. Mix in walnuts. Spread batter in greased 15½×10½×1-inch baking pan. Bake 20 to 25 minutes or until golden brown. Cool completely in pan on wire rack. Cut into bars.

Makes about 4 dozen bars

Pineapple Almond Shortbread Bars

Pineapple Almond Shortbread Bars

Crust

- 1½ cups all-purpose flour
- ½ cup DOLE® Almonds, toasted, ground
- ¼ cup sugar
- ½ cup cold margarine

Topping

- 1 can (20 ounces) DOLE® Crushed Pineapple, drained
- 3 eggs
- ¼ cup honey
- ¼ cup sugar
- 1 tablespoon grated lemon peel
- 1½ cups DOLE® Slivered Almonds, toasted

For Crust, preheat oven to 350°F. In large bowl, combine flour, almonds and sugar. Cut in margarine until crumbly. Form dough into a ball; press into ungreased 13×9-inch baking pan. Bake 10 minutes. Cool slightly.

For Topping, in medium bowl, combine pineapple, eggs, honey, sugar and lemon peel. Stir in almonds. Pour topping over partially baked crust. Bake an additional 30 to 35 minutes. Cool completely in pan on wire rack. Cut into bars.

Makes about 2 dozen bars

Molasses Applesauce Bars

½ cup butter or margarine, softened
1 cup granulated sugar
¼ cup dark molasses
2 eggs
2⅓ cups sifted flour
1 teaspoon baking soda
1 teaspoon ground cinnamon
½ teaspoon salt
½ teaspoon ground nutmeg
½ teaspoon ground ginger
1 cup applesauce
1 cup DEL MONTE® Seedless Raisins, chopped
1 tablespoon grated orange peel
Powdered sugar

Preheat oven to 350°F. In large bowl, cream butter and granulated sugar until light and fluffy. Add molasses and eggs; mix well. In medium bowl, sift together flour, baking soda, cinnamon, salt, nutmeg and ginger. Add flour mixture alternately with applesauce to creamed mixture, mixing well after each addition. Stir in raisins and orange peel. Spread into greased and floured 13×9-inch baking pan. Bake 25 to 30 minutes or until wooden toothpick inserted in center comes out clean. Cool completely in pan on wire rack. Sprinkle with powdered sugar. Cut into bars.

Makes about 3 dozen bars

Double Delicious Cookie Bars

Double Delicious Cookie Bars

½ cup margarine or butter
1½ cups graham cracker crumbs
1 (14-ounce) can EAGLE® Brand Sweetened Condensed Milk (NOT evaporated milk)
1 (12-ounce) package semi-sweet chocolate chips
1 cup peanut butter chips

Preheat oven to 350°F (325°F for glass dish). In 13×9-inch baking pan, melt margarine in oven. Sprinkle crumbs evenly over margarine; pour sweetened condensed milk evenly over crumbs. Top with chips; press down firmly. Bake 25 to 30 minutes or until lightly browned. Cool. Garnish as desired. Cut into bars. Store loosely covered at room temperature.

Makes 2 to 3 dozen bars

Variation: For drizzle-topped bars, melt 1 cup semi-sweet chocolate chips with 1½ teaspoons shortening. Drizzle over bars.

Double Chocolate Raspberry Bars

Bars

1¾ cups all-purpose flour
1 cup granulated sugar
¼ cup unsweetened cocoa powder
1 cup cold butter or margarine
1 egg, lightly beaten
1 teaspoon vanilla
1 can SOLO® or 1 jar BAKER® Raspberry Filling
1 cup chopped almonds or pecans
6 squares (1 ounce each) semi-sweet chocolate, finely chopped, or 1 package (6 ounces) semi-sweet chocolate morsels

Glaze

1 cup powdered sugar
1 to 2 tablespoons milk

Preheat oven to 350°F. Grease 13×9-inch baking pan; set aside.

For Bars, combine flour, granulated sugar and cocoa in medium bowl. Cut in butter until mixture resembles coarse crumbs. Add egg and vanilla; stir well. Set aside 1 cup cocoa mixture. Press remaining mixture into bottom of pan. Top with raspberry filling. Combine reserved cocoa mixture, almonds and chocolate. Sprinkle over filling. Bake 40 minutes. Cool completely in pan on wire rack.

For Glaze, combine powdered sugar and milk in small bowl; stir until smooth. Drizzle glaze in zig-zag pattern over cooled bars. Let stand until glaze is set. Cut into bars.

Makes about 3 dozen bars

Easy Apricot Oatmeal Bars

1½ cups all-purpose flour
¾ cup firmly packed brown sugar
1 teaspoon baking powder
1 cup cold butter or margarine
1½ cups quick-cooking rolled oats, uncooked
½ cup flaked coconut
½ cup coarsely chopped walnuts
1 can SOLO® or 1 jar BAKER® Apricot, Raspberry or Strawberry Filling

Preheat oven to 350°F. Grease 13×9-inch baking pan; set aside.

Combine flour, brown sugar and baking powder in medium bowl. Cut in butter until mixture resembles coarse crumbs. Add oats, coconut and walnuts; mix until crumbly. Press half of mixture into prepared pan. Spoon apricot filling over crumb mixture. Sprinkle remaining crumb mixture over apricot layer.

Bake 25 to 30 minutes or until lightly browned. (Center may seem soft but will set when cool.) Cool completely in pan on wire rack. Cut into bars.

Makes about 3 dozen bars

Top to bottom: Double Chocolate Raspberry Bars, Easy Apricot Oatmeal Bars

Chocolate Meringue Peanut Squares

Chocolate Meringue Peanut Squares

Crust

1½ cups all-purpose flour
½ cup sugar
¾ cup LAND O LAKES® Butter, softened
2 egg yolks, reserve egg whites
2 teaspoons vanilla

Filling

2 reserved egg whites
⅓ cup sugar
1 cup chopped salted peanuts
½ cup milk chocolate chips

Preheat oven 325°F. For Crust, in large mixer bowl, combine all crust ingredients. Beat at low speed, scraping bowl often, until mixture is crumbly, 1 to 2 minutes. Press onto bottom of greased 13×9×2-inch baking pan.

For Filling, in small bowl, beat egg whites at high speed, scraping bowl often, until soft mounds form, 1 to 2 minutes. Gradually add sugar; beat until stiff peaks form, 1 to 2 minutes. Fold in peanuts and chocolate chips. Spread over crust. Bake for 30 to 35 minutes, or until lightly browned. Cool completely in pan on wire rack. Cut into squares.
Makes about 3 dozen squares

Glazed Lemon Bars

Crust

1 cup sifted all-purpose flour
¼ cup confectioners sugar
¼ teaspoon salt
½ cup BUTTER FLAVOR CRISCO®

Filling

1 cup granulated sugar
2 tablespoons all-purpose flour
½ teaspoon baking powder
⅛ teaspoon salt
2 eggs, slightly beaten
2 tablespoons lemon juice
1 teaspoon grated lemon peel

Glaze

½ cup confectioners sugar
1 tablespoon BUTTER FLAVOR CRISCO®
1 tablespoon lemon juice
½ teaspoon grated lemon peel

1. Preheat oven to 325°F.

2. For Crust, combine flour, confectioners sugar and salt in medium bowl. Cut in BUTTER FLAVOR CRISCO® with pastry

blender or 2 knives until mixture is well blended. Press dough evenly in bottom of 9-inch square pan.

3. Bake 12 to 15 minutes or until lightly browned.

4. Meanwhile, for Filling, combine granulated sugar, flour, baking powder and salt in large bowl. Add eggs, lemon juice and peel; mix thoroughly.

5. Remove crust from oven; pour filling over crust.

6. Return to oven; bake for an additional 25 minutes.

7. For Glaze, combine all ingredients in small bowl. Remove pan from oven; spread glaze over filling. Cool completely in pan on wire rack. Cut into bars.

Makes about 2 dozen bars

Blueberry Cheesecake Bars

Blueberry Cheesecake Bars

1 package DUNCAN HINES® Bakery Style Blueberry Muffin Mix
¼ cup butter or margarine, softened
⅓ cup finely chopped pecans
1 package (8 ounces) cream cheese, softened
½ cup sugar
1 egg
3 tablespoons lemon juice
1 teaspoon grated lemon peel

1. Preheat oven to 350°F. Grease 9-inch square pan.

2. Rinse blueberries from mix with cold water and drain.

3. Place muffin mix in medium bowl. Cut in butter with pastry blender or two knives. Stir in pecans. Press into bottom of pan. Bake for 15 minutes or until set.

4. Combine cream cheese and sugar in medium bowl. Beat until smooth. Add egg, lemon juice and lemon peel. Beat well. Spread over baked crust. Sprinkle with blueberries. Sprinkle topping packet from mix over blueberries. Return to oven. Bake for an additional 35 to 40 minutes or until filling is set. Cool completely in pan on wire rack. Refrigerate until ready to serve. Cut into bars.

Makes about 16 bars

Crisp 'n' Crunchy Almond Coconut Bars, Strawberry Wonders

Crisp 'n' Crunchy Almond Coconut Bars

Crust

1¼ cups all-purpose flour
¼ cup granulated sugar
½ cup LAND O LAKES® Butter, softened
½ teaspoon rum extract
¼ cup sliced almonds, toasted

Filling

1 cup powdered sugar
¼ cup LAND O LAKES® Butter
¼ cup milk
2 tablespoons all-purpose flour
½ teaspoon rum extract
1 cup flaked coconut
1 cup sliced almonds

Preheat oven to 375°F. For Crust, in small mixer bowl, combine flour, granulated sugar, butter and rum extract. Beat at low speed, scraping bowl often, until mixture is crumbly, 1 to 2 minutes. Stir in nuts. Press on bottom of ungreased 9-inch square baking pan. Bake for 12 to 18 minutes, or until edges are lightly browned.

For Filling, in small saucepan, combine powdered sugar, butter, milk, flour and rum extract. Cook, stirring constantly, over medium heat until mixture comes to a full boil, 5 to 7 minutes. Stir in coconut and nuts. Pour over crust. Continue baking for 11 to 16 minutes, or until lightly browned. Cool completely in pan on wire rack. Cut into bars.

Makes about 2 dozen bars

74

Strawberry Wonders

Crust

1½ cups all-purpose flour
½ cup quick-cooking oats, uncooked
½ cup granulated sugar
¾ cup LAND O LAKES® Butter, softened
½ teaspoon baking soda

Topping

¾ cup flaked coconut
¾ cup chopped walnuts
¼ cup all-purpose flour
¼ cup firmly packed brown sugar
2 tablespoons LAND O LAKES® Butter, softened
½ teaspoon ground cinnamon
1 jar (10 ounces) strawberry preserves

Preheat oven to 350°F. For Crust, in large mixer bowl, combine all crust ingredients. Beat at low speed, scraping bowl often, until mixture is crumbly, 1 to 2 minutes. Press crust mixture on bottom of greased 13×9×2-inch baking pan. Bake for 18 to 22 minutes, or until edges are lightly browned.

For Topping, in same mixer bowl, combine coconut, nuts, flour, brown sugar, butter and cinnamon. Beat at low speed, scraping bowl often, until well mixed. Spread preserves to ¼ inch of edges of hot crust. Sprinkle topping mixture over preserves. Continue baking 18 to 22 minutes, or until edges are lightly browned. Cool completely in pan on wire rack. Cut into bars.

Makes about 3 dozen bars

Banana Split Bars

2 extra-ripe, medium DOLE® Bananas, peeled
2 cups all-purpose flour
1 cup granulated sugar
¾ teaspoon baking soda
½ teaspoon salt
½ teaspoon ground cinnamon
1 can (8 ounces) DOLE® Crushed Pineapple, undrained
2 eggs
½ cup vegetable oil
1 teaspoon vanilla extract
¼ cup maraschino cherries, drained, halved
Creamy Vanilla Frosting (recipe follows)

Preheat oven to 350°F. In food processor or blender container, process bananas until pureed (1 cup). In large bowl, combine flour, granulated sugar, baking soda, salt and cinnamon. Add pureed bananas, pineapple with juice, eggs, oil and vanilla. Mix until well blended. Stir in cherries. Pour into greased and floured 13×9-inch baking pan. Bake 30 to 35 minutes. Cool in pan on wire rack 30 minutes. Spread with Creamy Vanilla Frosting. Cut into bars.

Makes about 3 dozen bars

Creamy Vanilla Frosting

¼ cup margarine
3 to 4 tablespoons milk
3 cups powdered sugar
1 teaspoon vanilla extract

In small saucepan, heat margarine and milk until margarine melts. Remove from heat. Stir in powdered sugar and vanilla. Beat until smooth.

Layered Fruit Bars

1 cup BUTTER FLAVOR CRISCO®
**1 cup firmly packed brown
 sugar**
½ teaspoon vanilla
**2 cups all-purpose flour
 Dash salt**
**½ cup quick oats (not instant
 or old fashioned),
 uncooked**

Prepare desired filling. Set aside. Preheat oven to 375°F. Combine BUTTER FLAVOR CRISCO®, brown sugar and vanilla in large bowl. Beat at medium speed of electric mixer until well blended. Add flour and salt; mix at low speed until well blended. Reserve ½ cup mixture; press remaining mixture in bottom of ungreased 13×9×2-inch pan. Bake 10 minutes.

In small bowl, combine reserved ½ cup mixture and oats; mix until crumbly. Spread desired filling evenly over baked base. Evenly sprinkle oat mixture over filling. Bake about 15 minutes, or until bubbly (or until set, for lime-cream cheese filling). Cool completely in pan on wire rack. Cut into 3×1½-inch bars.

Makes 2 dozen bars

Fillings:

Lime-Cream Cheese:
Combine 8 ounces softened cream cheese, 2 tablespoons lime juice, 1 egg and ½ cup granulated sugar in medium bowl. Beat at low speed of electric mixer until smooth. Spread over baked crust.

Pineapple-Coconut:
Combine 2 (8-ounce) cans crushed pineapple, undrained, ½ cup granulated sugar and 1 tablespoon cornstarch in medium saucepan. Cook and stir over medium heat until mixture comes to a boil and thickens. Stir in ¼ cup chopped pecans, ½ cup flaked coconut and 1 teaspoon lemon juice. Spread over baked crust.

Blueberry:
Spread 1 can (21 ounces) blueberry pie filling over baked crust.

Double Chocolate Fantasy Bars

**1 (18¼- or 18½-ounce)
 package chocolate
 cake mix**
⅓ cup vegetable oil
1 egg
1 cup chopped nuts
**1 (14-ounce) can EAGLE®
 Brand Sweetened
 Condensed Milk (NOT
 evaporated milk)**
**1 cup (6 ounces) semi-sweet
 chocolate chips**
**1 teaspoon vanilla extract
 Dash salt**

Preheat oven to 350°F. In large mixer bowl, combine cake mix, oil and egg; beat on medium speed until crumbly. Stir in nuts. Reserving 1½ cups crumb mixture, press remainder firmly on bottom of greased 13×9-inch baking pan. In small saucepan, combine remaining ingredients. Over medium heat, cook and stir until chips melt. Pour evenly over prepared crust. Top with reserved crumb mixture. Bake 25 to 30 minutes or until bubbly. Cool. Cut into bars. Store loosely covered at room temperature.

Makes 2 to 3 dozen bars

Chocolate Macaroon Squares

Topping
One 14-ounce can
    CARNATION® Sweetened
    Condensed Milk
1 teaspoon vanilla extract
1 egg
One 3½-ounce can (1⅓ cups)
    flaked coconut, divided
1 cup chopped pecans
One 6-ounce package (1 cup)
    NESTLE® Toll House®
    Semi-Sweet Chocolate
    Morsels

Base
One 18½-ounce package
    chocolate cake mix
⅓ cup butter, softened
1 egg

For Topping, in large bowl,
combine sweetened
condensed milk, vanilla extract
and egg; beat until well
blended. Stir in 1 cup coconut,
pecans and NESTLE® Toll House®
Semi-Sweet Chocolate Morsels.
Set aside.

For Base, preheat oven to 350°F.
In large bowl, combine cake
mix, butter and egg; mix until
crumbly. Press into greased
13×9-inch baking pan.

Spread topping over base.
Sprinkle remaining ⅓ cup
coconut over top. Bake 30 to
40 minutes. Center may appear
loose but will set upon cooling.
Cool completely in pan on wire
rack. Cut into squares.
    Makes about 2 dozen squares

Peanut Butter Bars

1 package DUNCAN HINES®
    Peanut Butter Cookie Mix
2 egg whites
½ cup chopped peanuts
1 cup confectioners sugar
2 tablespoons water
½ teaspoon vanilla extract

1. Preheat oven to 350°F.

2. Combine cookie mix, peanut
butter packet from mix and
egg whites in large bowl. Stir
until thoroughly blended. Press
into ungreased 13×9×2-inch
pan. Sprinkle peanuts over
dough. Press lightly.

3. Bake 16 to 18 minutes or until
golden brown. Cool completely
in pan on wire rack. Combine
confectioners sugar, water and
vanilla extract in small bowl. Stir
until blended. Drizzle glaze over
top. Cut into bars.
    Makes about 2 dozen bars

Peanut Butter Bars

Orange Butter Cream Squares

Crust

1¼ cups finely crushed chocolate wafer cookies
⅓ cup LAND O LAKES® Butter, softened

Filling

1½ cups powdered sugar
⅓ cup LAND O LAKES® Butter, softened
1 tablespoon milk
2 teaspoons grated orange peel
½ teaspoon vanilla

Glaze

1 tablespoon unsweetened cocoa
1 tablespoon LAND O LAKES® Butter, melted

For Crust, in medium bowl, stir together cookie crumbs and butter. Press on bottom of ungreased 9-inch square baking pan. Refrigerate until firm, about 1 hour.

For Filling, in small mixer bowl, combine all filling ingredients. Beat at medium speed, scraping bowl often until light and fluffy, 3 to 4 minutes. Spread over crust.

For Glaze, in small bowl, stir together cocoa and butter. Drizzle over filling. Refrigerate until firm, about 2 hours. Cut into bars. Store in refrigerator.

Makes about 2 dozen bars

Chocolate Chip Raisin Bars

Prep time: 10 minutes
Chill time: 15 minutes
Bake time: 20 minutes

1½ cups firmly packed brown sugar
¾ cup margarine, softened
2 eggs
2 teaspoons vanilla extract
2 cups all-purpose flour
1 teaspoon baking soda
1 cup semi-sweet chocolate chips
1 cup DOLE® Raisins
Powdered sugar (optional)

Preheat oven to 375°F. In large bowl, beat brown sugar and margarine until light and fluffy. Beat in eggs and vanilla until blended.

In medium bowl, combine flour and baking soda. Beat into creamed mixture until well blended. Stir in chocolate chips and raisins. Refrigerate, covered, for 15 minutes.

Press batter into 13×9-inch baking pan. Bake 18 to 20 minutes. (Bars will appear slightly underbaked.) Cool slightly. Cut into bars while warm. Cool completely in pan on wire rack. Dust with powdered sugar, if desired.

Makes about 16 bars

Orange Butter Cream Squares

Heath® Bars

1 cup butter, softened
1 cup firmly packed brown sugar
1 egg yolk
1 teaspoon vanilla
2 cups flour
2 (6-ounce) bags HEATH® Bits, divided
½ cup finely chopped pecans

Preheat oven to 350°F. In large bowl, with electric mixer, cream butter well; blend in brown sugar, egg yolk and vanilla. By hand, mix in flour, 1½ bags HEATH® Bits and nuts. Press into ungreased 15½×10½-inch jelly-roll pan.

Bake 18 to 20 minutes, or until browned. Remove from oven and immediately sprinkle remaining ½ bag HEATH® Bits over top. Cool slightly; cut into bars while warm.

Makes about 4 dozen bars

Heath® Bars

Chocolate-Frosted Almond Shortbread

¾ cup butter, softened
¼ cup firmly packed light brown sugar
¼ cup powdered sugar
1 egg yolk
1 teaspoon almond extract
1½ cups all-purpose flour
⅛ teaspoon baking soda
7 ounces (about 1 cup) almond paste
½ cup granulated sugar
1 egg
½ cup milk chocolate chips

Preheat oven to 350°F. Cover bottom of 9-inch pie pan with parchment or waxed paper.

Cream butter, brown sugar, powdered sugar, egg yolk and almond extract in large bowl. Blend in flour and baking soda until smooth. Press half of dough into prepared pie pan. Beat almond paste, granulated sugar and whole egg in small bowl until smooth. Spread over dough in pan. Roll out remaining half of dough on lightly floured surface into a circle to fit top of almond layer. Place over almond layer; press down to smooth top.

Bake 30 to 40 minutes or until top appears very lightly browned and feels firm. Remove from oven; sprinkle chocolate chips over top. Let stand a few minutes until chips melt, then spread evenly over shortbread. Refrigerate until chocolate is set. Cut into slim wedges to serve.

Makes 16 to 20 bars

"Cordially Yours" Chocolate Chip Bars

"Cordially Yours" Chocolate Chip Bars

¾ cup **BUTTER FLAVOR CRISCO**®
2 eggs
½ cup granulated sugar
¼ cup firmly packed brown
    sugar
1½ teaspoons vanilla extract
1 teaspoon almond extract
2 cups all-purpose flour
1 teaspoon baking soda
½ teaspoon ground cinnamon
1 can (21 ounces) cherry pie
    filling
1½ cups milk chocolate
    big chips
    Powdered sugar

1. Preheat oven to 350°F. Grease
15½×10½×1-inch pan with BUTTER
FLAVOR CRISCO®.

2. Combine BUTTER FLAVOR
CRISCO®, eggs, granulated
sugar, brown sugar, vanilla and
almond extract in large bowl.
Beat at medium speed of
electric mixer until well blended.

3. Combine flour, baking soda
and cinnamon. Mix into
creamed mixture at low speed
until just blended. Stir in pie
filling and chocolate chips
with spoon. Spread in pan.

4. Bake 25 minutes, or until lightly
browned and top springs back
when lightly pressed. Cool
completely in pan on cooling
rack. Sprinkle with powdered
sugar. Cut into bars.
    Makes about 2½ dozen bars

Apple Pie Bars

Apple Pie Bars

Crust

    Milk
- **1 egg yolk, reserve egg white**
- **2½ cups all-purpose flour**
- **1 teaspoon salt**
- **1 cup cold LAND O LAKES® Butter**

Filling

- **1 cup crushed cornflake cereal**
- **8 cups peeled, cored, ¼-inch sliced, tart cooking apples (about 8 to 10 medium)**
- **1 cup granulated sugar**
- **1½ teaspoons ground cinnamon**
- **½ teaspoon ground nutmeg**
- **1 reserved egg white**
- **2 tablespoons granulated sugar**
- **½ teaspoon ground cinnamon**

Glaze

- **1 cup powdered sugar**
- **1 to 2 tablespoons milk**
- **½ teaspoon vanilla**

Preheat oven to 350°F. For Crust, add enough milk to egg yolk to measure ⅔ cup; set aside. In medium bowl, combine flour and salt. Cut in butter until crumbly. With fork, stir in milk mixture until dough forms a ball; divide into halves. Roll out half of the dough, on lightly floured surface, into a 15×10-inch rectangle. Place on bottom of ungreased 15×10×1-inch jelly-roll pan.

For Filling, sprinkle cereal over top of crust; layer apples over cereal. In small bowl, combine 1 cup granulated sugar, 1½ teaspoons cinnamon and nutmeg. Sprinkle over apples. Roll remaining half of dough into a 15½×10½-inch rectangle; place over apples. In small bowl, beat egg white with fork until foamy; brush over top crust. In another small bowl, stir together 2 tablespoons granulated sugar and ½ teaspoon cinnamon; sprinkle over top crust. Bake for 45 to 60 minutes or until lightly browned.

For Glaze, in small bowl, stir together all glaze ingredients. Drizzle over top crust while still warm. Cut into bars.

Makes about 3 dozen bars

Pumpkin Cheesecake Bars

- 1 (16-ounce) package pound cake mix
- 3 eggs
- 2 tablespoons margarine or butter, melted
- 4 teaspoons pumpkin pie spice
- 1 (8-ounce) package cream cheese, softened
- 1 (14-ounce) can EAGLE® Brand Sweetened Condensed Milk (NOT evaporated milk)
- 1 (16-ounce) can pumpkin (about 2 cups)
- ½ teaspoon salt
- 1 cup chopped nuts

Preheat oven to 350°F. In large mixer bowl on low speed, combine cake mix, *1 egg*, margarine and *2 teaspoons* pumpkin pie spice until crumbly. Press onto bottom of 15×10-inch baking pan. In large mixer bowl, beat cheese until fluffy. Gradually beat in sweetened condensed milk, remaining *2 eggs*, pumpkin, remaining *2 teaspoons* pumpkin pie spice and salt; mix well. Pour over crust; sprinkle with nuts. Bake 30 to 35 minutes or until set. Cool. Refrigerate; cut into bars. Store covered in refrigerator.

Makes 3 to 4 dozen bars

Pear Blondies

- 1 cup firmly packed brown sugar
- ¼ cup butter or margarine, melted
- 1 egg
- ½ teaspoon vanilla
- ¾ cup all-purpose flour
- ½ teaspoon baking powder
- ½ teaspoon salt
- 1 cup chopped firm-ripe fresh U.S.A. Anjou, Bosc, Bartlett, Nelis or Seckel pears
- ⅓ cup semi-sweet chocolate chips

Preheat oven to 350°F. In medium bowl, mix brown sugar, butter, egg and vanilla; blend well. In small bowl, combine flour, baking powder and salt; stir into brown sugar mixture. Stir in pears and chips. Spread in greased 8-inch square pan. Bake 30 to 35 minutes or until golden brown. Cool completely in pan on wire rack. Cut into 2-inch squares.

Makes 16 squares

Favorite recipe from **Oregon Washington California Pear Bureau**

Pumpkin Cheesecake Bars

Chocolatey Peanut Butter Goodies

Cookies

    1 cup BUTTER FLAVOR CRISCO®
    4 cups (1 pound) powdered sugar
    1½ cups JIF® Extra Crunchy Peanut Butter
    1½ cups graham cracker crumbs

Frosting

    1 tablespoon BUTTER FLAVOR CRISCO®
    1⅓ cups semi-sweet chocolate chips

1. For Cookies, combine BUTTER FLAVOR CRISCO®, powdered sugar, JIF® Extra Crunchy Peanut Butter and crumbs in large bowl with spoon. Spread evenly on bottom of 13×9-inch pan.

2. For Frosting, combine BUTTER FLAVOR CRISCO® and chocolate chips in small microwave-safe bowl. Microwave at MEDIUM (50%) for 1 minute; stir. Repeat until smooth (or melt on rangetop in small saucepan on very low heat). Spread over top of cookie mixture. Cool at least 1 hour, or until chocolate hardens. Cut into 2×1½-inch bars.   *Makes 3 dozen bars*

P. B. Graham Snackers

    ½ cup BUTTER FLAVOR CRISCO®
    2 cups powdered sugar
    ¾ cup JIF® Creamy Peanut Butter
    1 cup graham cracker crumbs
    ½ cup semi-sweet chocolate chips
    ½ cup graham cracker crumbs, crushed peanuts or chocolate sprinkles (optional)

1. Combine BUTTER FLAVOR CRISCO®, powdered sugar and JIF® Creamy Peanut Butter in large bowl. Beat at low speed of electric mixer until well blended. Stir in 1 cup crumbs and chocolate chips. Cover. Refrigerate 1 hour.

2. Form dough into 1-inch balls. Roll in ½ cup crumbs for a fancier cookie. Cover. Refrigerate until ready to serve.
    Makes about 3 dozen cookies

Top to bottom: P. B. Graham Snackers, Chocolatey Peanut Butter Goodies

Crunch Crowned Brownies

Crunch Crowned Brownies

1 package (21 to 23 ounces) fudge brownie mix
1 cup chopped nuts
⅔ cup quick oats, uncooked
½ cup firmly packed light brown sugar
¼ cup margarine, melted
1 teaspoon ground cinnamon
1½ cups "M&M's"® Plain Chocolate Candies

Preheat oven to 350°F. Prepare brownie mix according to package directions for cake-like brownies; spread batter into greased 13×9-inch baking pan. In large bowl, combine nuts, oats, brown sugar, margarine and cinnamon; mix well. Stir candies into nut mixture; sprinkle over batter. Bake 40 to 45 minutes. Cool completely on wire rack. Cut into squares.

Makes about 2½ dozen brownies

Pudding Drop Cookies

¾ cup sugar
2 eggs
¼ cup BLUE BONNET®
    Margarine, melted
1 cup all-purpose flour
1 (4-serving size) package
    ROYAL® Instant
    Butterscotch Pudding &
    Pie Filling*
½ cup chopped walnuts
½ cup semi-sweet chocolate
    chips

Preheat oven to 375°F. In medium bowl with electric mixer at high speed, beat sugar and eggs until thick and pale yellow. Beat in margarine until smooth. Stir in flour and pudding mix until blended. Stir in walnuts and chocolate chips. Drop batter by tablespoonfuls, 2 inches apart, onto greased and floured cookie sheets.

Bake 10 to 12 minutes or until lightly browned. Cool slightly on cookie sheets. Remove from cookie sheets; cool completely on wire racks. Store in airtight container.

Makes about 2 dozen cookies

*One (4-serving size) package ROYAL® Instant Chocolate or Vanilla Pudding and Pie Filling may be substituted.

Haystacks

2 cups butterscotch-flavored
    chips
½ cup JIF® Creamy Peanut
    Butter
¼ cup BUTTER FLAVOR CRISCO®
6 cups corn flakes
⅔ cup semi-sweet miniature
    chocolate chips
    Chopped peanuts or
    chocolate jimmies
    (optional)

1. Combine butterscotch chips, JIF® Creamy Peanut Butter and BUTTER FLAVOR CRISCO® in large microwave-safe bowl. Cover with waxed paper. Microwave at MEDIUM (50%) for 1 minute; stir. Repeat until smooth (or melt on rangetop in small saucepan on very low heat, stirring constantly).

2. Pour corn flakes into large bowl. Pour hot butterscotch mixture over flakes. Stir with spoon until flakes are coated. Stir in chocolate chips.

3. Spoon scant ¼ cupfuls of mixture into mounds on waxed paper-lined cookie sheets. Sprinkle with chopped nuts, if desired. Refrigerate until firm.

Makes about 3 dozen cookies

Buttery Jam Tarts

2½ cups all-purpose flour
½ cup sugar
⅔ cup LAND O LAKES® Butter, softened
1 egg
¼ teaspoon baking soda
¼ teaspoon salt
2 tablespoons milk
1 teaspoon almond extract
¾ cup cherry preserves
Sugar for sprinkling

Preheat oven to 350°F. In large mixer bowl, combine flour, ½ cup sugar, butter, egg, baking soda, salt, milk and almond extract. Beat at low speed, scraping bowl often, until well mixed, 3 to 4 minutes. Roll out dough, half at a time, on well-floured surface, to ⅛-inch thickness. Cut out with 2½-inch round cookie cutter. Place half of the cookies 2 inches apart on ungreased cookie sheets. Place level teaspoonfuls of cherry preserves in center of each cookie. Make small X or a cutout with a very small cookie cutter in top of each remaining cookie; place over each cookie with jam. Press together around edges with fork. Sprinkle with sugar. Bake for 11 to 13 minutes, or until edges are very lightly browned. Remove immediately; cool on wire racks.

Makes about 2 dozen cookies

Peanut Butter Chips and Jelly Bars

1½ cups all-purpose flour
½ cup sugar
¾ teaspoon baking powder
½ cup (1 stick) cold butter or margarine
1 egg, beaten
¾ cup grape jelly
1⅔ cups (10-ounce package) REESE'S® Peanut Butter Chips, divided

Preheat oven to 375°F. Grease 9-inch square baking pan.

In large bowl, stir together flour, sugar and baking powder; with pastry blender or fork, cut in butter until mixture resembles coarse crumbs. Add egg; blend well. Reserve half of mixture; press remaining mixture onto bottom of prepared pan. Spread jelly evenly over crust. Sprinkle 1 cup peanut butter chips over jelly. Stir together remaining crumb mixture with remaining ⅔ cup chips; sprinkle over top.

Bake 25 to 30 minutes or until bars are lightly browned. Cool completely in pan on wire rack; cut into bars.

Makes about 1½ dozen bars

Buttery Jam Tarts

Granola Apple Cookies

1 cup firmly packed brown
 sugar
¾ cup margarine or butter,
 softened
1 egg
¾ cup MOTT'S® Natural Apple
 Sauce
1 teaspoon vanilla
3 cups granola with dates
 and raisins
1½ cups all-purpose flour
1 teaspoon baking powder
1 teaspoon ground cinnamon
½ teaspoon baking soda
½ teaspoon salt
½ teaspoon ground allspice
1 cup flaked coconut
1 cup unsalted sunflower nuts

In large bowl, combine brown
sugar, margarine, egg, apple
sauce and vanilla; beat well. Stir
in remaining ingredients; mix
well. Refrigerate 1 to 2 hours for
ease in handling.

Preheat oven to 375°F. Grease
cookie sheets. Drop dough by
teaspoonfuls 2 inches apart
onto prepared cookie sheets.
Bake 11 to 13 minutes or until
edges are light golden brown.
Immediately remove from
cookie sheets. Cool on wire
racks. Store cookies in airtight
container to retain their soft,
chewy texture.
 Makes about 5 dozen cookies

Variation: For larger cookies,
drop ¼ cupfuls of dough onto
greased cookie sheets; press
lightly to flatten. Bake at 375°F
for 13 to 15 minutes. Cool on wire
racks.

Oreo® Brownie Treats

Oreo® Brownie Treats

1 (21½-ounce) package
 deluxe fudge brownie mix
15 OREO® Chocolate Sandwich
 Cookies, coarsely
 chopped
2 pints ice cream, any flavor
 (optional)

Prepare fudge brownie mix
according to package
directions; stir in cookies. Grease
bottom of 13×9×2-inch baking
pan; pour batter into pan.
Bake according to package
directions. Cool on wire rack.
Cut into 12 squares. To serve, top
each brownie with scoop of ice
cream, if desired.
 Makes 1 dozen brownies

Teddy Wants S'Mores

9 NABISCO® Grahams, cut in
   half
8 ounces milk chocolate
2 cups Honey, Cinnamon
   or Chocolate
   TEDDY GRAHAMS® Graham
   Snacks, divided
1½ cups miniature
   marshmallows

Grease and waxed paper-line 8×8×2-inch baking pan. Cover bottom of pan with graham cracker halves; set aside.

In small saucepan over very low heat, melt chocolate. Remove from heat. Stir in 1½ cups TEDDY GRAHAMS® and marshmallows. Spread mixture evenly over graham cracker halves. Press remaining TEDDY GRAHAMS® on top of chocolate mixture. Let stand until firm. Cut into bars.

Makes about 1½ dozen bars

Giant Raisin-Chip Frisbees

1 cup butter or margarine,
   softened
1 cup firmly packed brown
   sugar
½ cup granulated sugar
2 eggs
1 teaspoon vanilla
1½ cups all-purpose flour
¼ cup unsweetened cocoa
1 teaspoon baking soda
1 cup (6 ounces) semi-sweet
   chocolate chips
¾ cup raisins
¾ cup chopped walnuts

Preheat oven to 350°F. Line cookie sheets with parchment paper or lightly grease and dust with flour. Cream butter with sugars in large bowl. Add eggs and vanilla; beat until light. Combine flour, cocoa and baking soda in small bowl. Add to creamed mixture with chocolate chips, raisins and walnuts; stir until well blended. Scoop out about ½ cupful of dough for each cookie. Place on cookie sheets, spacing about 5 inches apart. Using knife dipped in water, smooth dough out to 3½ inches in diameter. Bake 10 to 12 minutes or until golden. Remove to wire racks to cool.

Makes about 16 cookies

Magic Cookie Bars

½ cup margarine or butter
1½ cups graham cracker
   crumbs
1 (14-ounce) can EAGLE®
   Brand Sweetened
   Condensed Milk
   (NOT evaporated milk)
1 cup (6 ounces) semi-sweet
   chocolate chips
1 (3½-ounce) can flaked
   coconut (1⅓ cups)
1 cup chopped walnuts

Preheat oven to 350°F (325°F for glass dish). In 13×9-inch baking pan, melt margarine in oven. Sprinkle crumbs over margarine; pour sweetened condensed milk evenly over crumbs. Top with remaining ingredients; press down firmly. Bake 25 to 30 minutes or until lightly browned. Cool. Refrigerate if desired. Cut into bars. Store loosely covered at room temperature.

Makes 2 to 3 dozen bars

Cookie Pizza

Cookie Pizza

**1 package (20 ounces)
refrigerated sugar cookie
dough
1 box (5.4 ounces) SUNKIST®
FUN FRUITS®–Assorted Fruit
Snacks (any variety)
Assorted icings, colored
sugar crystals and decors,
for garnish**

Preheat oven to 350°F. Line 12- or 14-inch pizza pan with aluminum foil. Spray with nonstick cooking spray; press cookie dough evenly into pan. Press fruit snacks into pizza in decorative design. Bake 20 minutes or until cookie edges are golden brown. Cool 10 minutes on wire rack. Remove cookie from pan; discard foil. Decorate as desired. Cut into wedges to serve.

Makes about 8 servings

Favorite recipe from **Thomas J. Lipton Company**

Tony's Tiger Bites™

**1 package (10 ounces)
regular-size marshmallows
(about 40)
¼ cup margarine
⅓ cup peanut butter
7½ cups (10-ounce package)
KELLOGG'S FROSTED
FLAKES® Cereal**

1. In 4-quart microwave-safe bowl, cook marshmallows and margarine at HIGH (100%) 3 minutes or until melted, stirring after 1½ minutes.

2. Stir in peanut butter until mixture is smooth. Add KELLOGG'S FROSTED FLAKES cereal, stirring until well coated.

3. Using a buttered spatula or waxed paper, press mixture into a 13×9×2-inch pan coated with nonstick cooking spray. Cool; cut into bars.

Makes about 32 bars

Note: Use fresh marshmallows for best results.

Rangetop Directions: Melt margarine over low heat in large saucepan. Add marshmallows, stirring until completely melted. Remove from heat. Follow steps 2 and 3 above.

ACKNOWLEDGMENTS

**The publishers would like to thank
the companies and organizations listed below for
the use of their recipes in this publication.**

Arm & Hammer Division, Church & Dwight Co., Inc.
Best Foods, a Division of CPC International Inc.
Blue Diamond Growers
Borden Kitchens, Borden, Inc.
Carnation, Nestle Food Company
Del Monte Foods
Diamond Walnut Growers, Inc.
Dole Food Company, Inc.
Hershey Chocolate U.S.A.
Kellogg Company
Kraft General Foods, Inc.
Land O'Lakes, Inc.
Leaf, Inc.
Thomas J. Lipton Co.

M&M/Mars
Mott's U.S.A., A division of Cadbury Beverages Inc.
Nabisco Foods Group
Nestle Chocolate and Confection Company
Norseland Foods, Inc.
Oregon Washington California Pear Bureau
The Procter & Gamble Company, Inc.
The Quaker Oats Company
The J.M. Smucker Company
Sokol and Company
Sunkist Growers, Inc.
Sun•Maid Growers of California

PHOTO CREDITS

**The publishers would like to thank
the companies and organizations listed below for
the use of their photographs in this publication.**

Borden Kitchens, Borden, Inc.
Dole Food Company, Inc.
Hershey Chocolate U.S.A.
Land O'Lakes, Inc.
Leaf, Inc.
Thomas J. Lipton Co.
Nabisco Foods Group

Nestle Chocolate and Confection Company
Norseland Foods, Inc.
The Procter & Gamble Company, Inc.
Sunkist Growers, Inc.

INDEX

A

All American Heath® Brownies, 35
Almond Cream Cheese Cookies, 45
Almond Fudge Cups, 48
Apple Pie Bars, 82
Apple Sauce Brownies, 39
Austrian Tea Cookies, 48

B

Banana Cookies, 19
Banana Orange Softies, 8
Banana Split Bars, 75
Bar Cookies (see also **Brownies**)
  Apple Pie Bars, 82
  Banana Split Bars, 75
  Blueberry Cheesecake Bars, 73
  Chewy Bar Cookies, 68
  Chocolate Chip Raisin Bars, 78
  Chocolate-Frosted Almond
    Shortbread, 80
  Chocolate Macaroon Squares, 77
  Chocolate Meringue Peanut
    Squares, 72

Bar Cookies (continued)
  Chocolatey Peanut Butter
    Goodies, 84
  "Cordially Yours" Chocolate Chip
    Bars, 81
  Crisp 'n' Crunchy Almond
    Coconut Bars, 74
  Double Chocolate Fantasy
    Bars, 76
  Double Chocolate Raspberry
    Bars, 71
  Double Delicious Cookie Bars, 69
  Easy Apricot Oatmeal Bars, 71
  Glazed Lemon Bars, 72
  Heath® Bars, 80
  Layered Fruit Bars, 76
  Magic Cookie Bars, 91
  Molasses Applesauce Bars, 69
  Oatmeal Scotchie Pan
    Cookies, 57
  Orange Butter Cream Squares, 78
  Peanut Butter Bars, 77
  Peanut Butter Chips and Jelly
    Bars, 88
  Pear Blondies, 83
  Pineapple Almond Shortbread
    Bars, 68
  Pumpkin Cheesecake Bars, 83
  Strawberry Wonders, 75
  Teddy Wants S'Mores, 91
  Toffee-Bran Bars, 66
  Toll House® Pan Cookies, 60
  Tony's Tiger Bites™, 92
Best Brownies, 36
Bittersweet Brownies, 33
Black Forest Oatmeal Fancies, 55
Blonde Brickle Brownies, 26
Blueberry Cheesecake Bars, 73
Blueberry Drop Cookies, 15
Brownies
  All American Heath® Brownies, 35
  Apple Sauce Brownies, 39
  Best Brownies, 36
  Bittersweet Brownies, 33
  Blonde Brickle Brownies, 26
  Brownie Pizza, 36
  Butterscotch Brownies, 33
  Chocolate-Mint Brownies, 28
  Cranberry Orange Ricotta
    Cheese Brownies, 24
  Crunch Crowned Brownies, 86
  Decadent Brownies, 27
  Double "Topped" Brownies, 34
  Fancy Walnut Brownies, 29
  German Chocolate Brownies, 27
  Irish Coffee Brownies, 30
  Oreo® Brownie Treats, 90
  Peanut Butter Chip Brownies, 32
  Quick No-Bake Brownies, 28
  Raspberry Fudge Brownies, 38
  Rocky Road Brownies, 30
  Supreme Chocolate Saucepan
    Brownies, 39
  Ultimate Brownies, 35
  White Chocolate Brownies, 26
Butterscotch Brownies, 33
Buttery Jam Tarts, 88

C

Chewy Bar Cookies, 68
Choco-Dipped Peanut Butter
  Cookies, 12
Chocolate
  Almond Fudge Cups, 48
  Chocolate Cherry Cookies, 51
  Chocolate Glaze, 28
  Chocolate Macaroon Squares, 77
  Chocolate Oat Chewies, 9
  Chocolate Peanut Butter Chip
    Cookies, 57
  Chocolatey Peanut Butter
    Goodies, 84
  Double Chocolate Fantasy
    Bars, 76
  Drizzle, 62
  Fudge Glaze, 27
  Ice Cream Cookies, 50
  Orange Butter Cream Squares, 78
  Peanut Blossoms, 12
  Raspberry-Filled Chocolate
    Ravioli, 42
  Teddy Wants S'Mores, 91
  Toffee-Bran Bars, 66
Chocolate Almond Snowballs, 12
Chocolate Biscotti, 50
Chocolate Chips
  Black Forest Oatmeal Fancies, 55
  Chocolate Chip Cordials, 47
  Chocolate Chip Oatmeal Raisin
    Cookies, 62
  Chocolate Chip Raisin Bars, 78
  Chocolate Dipped Ultimate
    Chocolate Chip Cookies, 63
  Chocolate Macaroon Squares, 77
  Chocolate Meringue Peanut
    Squares, 72
  "Cordially Yours" Chocolate Chip
    Bars, 81
  Double Chocolate Chip
    Cookies, 59
  Double Chocolate Raspberry
    Bars, 71
  Double Delicious Cookie Bars, 69
  Double Nut Chocolate Chip
    Cookies, 65
  Forgotten Chips Cookies, 58
  Giant Raisin-Chip Frisbees, 91
  Heavenly Almond Treats, 60
  Hershey's® More Chips Chocolate
    Chip Cookies, 64
  Magic Cookie Bars, 91
  Original Toll House® Chocolate
    Chip Cookies, 60
  Peanut Butter Chip Brownies, 32
  Reese's™ Cookies, 18
  Rocky Road Brownies, 30
  San Francisco Cookies, 54
  Supreme Chocolate Saucepan
    Brownies, 39
  Toll House® Pan Cookies, 60
  Ultimate Brownies, 35
  Ultimate Chocolate Chip
    Cookies, 62
  Whole Grain Chippers, 54

Chocolate Cut-Out Cookies, 51
Chocolate-Dipped Brandy
	Snaps, 43
Chocolate-Frosted Almond
	Shortbread, 80
Chocolate-Mint Brownies, 28
Chocolate Refrigerator Cookies, 6
Chocolate Rum Balls, 46
Cocoa
	Chocolate Almond Snowballs, 12
	Chocolate Biscotti, 50
	Chocolate Cut-Out Cookies, 51
	Chocolate Refrigerator Cookies, 6
	Chocolate Rum Balls, 46
	Cocoa Snickerdoodles, 19
	Creamy Brownie Frosting, 36
	Double Chocolate Raspberry
		Bars, 71
	Giant Raisin-Chip Frisbees, 91
	Greeting Card Cookies, 40
	Hershey's® Vanilla Chip Chocolate
		Cookies, 63
	Ivory Chip Strawberry Fudge
		Drops, 52
	No-Bake Peanutty Chocolate
		Drops, 20
Cookie Pizza, 92

Cookies from Mixes
	Blueberry Cheesecake Bars, 73
	Brownie Pizza, 36
	Chocolate Chip Cordials, 47
	Chocolate Chip Oatmeal Raisin
		Cookies, 62
	Chocolate Oat Chewies, 9
	Crunch Crowned Brownies, 86
	Double Chocolate Fantasy
		Bars, 76
	Double Nut Chocolate Chip
		Cookies, 65
	Double "Topped" Brownies, 34
	Fancy Walnut Brownies, 29
	German Chocolate Brownies, 27
	Lemon Cookies, 20
	Oreo® Brownie Treats, 90
	Peanut Butter Jewels, 18
	Pumpkin Cheesecake Bars, 83
	Ultimate Brownies, 35
	White Chocolate Brownies, 26

"Cordially Yours" Chocolate Chip
	Bars, 81
Cranberry Orange Ricotta Cheese
	Brownies, 24
Creamy Brownie Frosting, 36
Creamy Vanilla Frosting, 75
Crisp 'n' Crunchy Almond Coconut
	Bars, 74
Crunch Crowned Brownies, 86

D

Decadent Brownies, 27
Decorative Frosting, 40
Double Chocolate Chip
	Cookies, 59
Double Chocolate Fantasy Bars, 76
Double Chocolate Raspberry
	Bars, 71
Double Delicious Cookie Bars, 69
Double Nut Chocolate Chip
	Cookies, 65
Double "Topped" Brownies, 34
Drizzle, 62
Drop Cookies
	Banana Cookies, 19
	Banana Orange Softies, 8
	Black Forest Oatmeal Fancies, 55
	Blueberry Drop Cookies, 15
	Chocolate Chip Cordials, 47
	Chocolate Dipped Ultimate
		Chocolate Chip Cookies, 63
	Cocoa Snickerdoodles, 19
	Double Chocolate Chip
		Cookies, 59
	Drop Sugar Cookies, 20
	Forgotten Chips Cookies, 58
	Giant Raisin-Chip Frisbees, 91
	Ginger Snap Oats, 16
	Granola Apple Cookies, 90
	Haystacks, 87
	Heavenly Almond Treats, 60
	Hershey's® More Chips Chocolate
		Chip Cookies, 64
	Hershey's® Vanilla Chip Chocolate
		Cookies, 63
	Ivory Chip Strawberry Fudge
		Drops, 52
	Maple Raisin Cookies, 23
	Marvelous Macaroons, 6
	Mom's Best Oatmeal Cookies, 16
	No-Bake Peanutty Chocolate
		Drops, 20
	Oatmeal Apple Cookies, 22
	Oatmeal Scotchies, 57
	Original Toll House® Chocolate
		Chip Cookies, 60
	Peanut Butter Sunshine
		Cookies, 64
	Pudding Drop Cookies, 87
	Reese's™ Cookies, 18
	San Francisco Cookies, 54
	Spicy Pumpkin Cookies, 47
	Tropical Orange Coconut
		Drops, 15

Drop Cookies (*continued*)
	Ultimate Chocolate Chip
		Cookies, 62
	Whole Wheat Oatmeal Cookies, 8

E

Easy Apricot Oatmeal Bars, 71
Easy Peanut Butter Cookies, 12
Easy Peanutty Snickerdoodles, 59

F

Fancy Walnut Brownies, 29
Forgotten Chips Cookies, 58
Fruit Burst Cookies, 22
Fudge Glaze, 27

G

German Chocolate Brownies, 27
Giant Raisin-Chip Frisbees, 91
Ginger Snap Oats, 16
Glazed Lemon Bars, 72
Granola Apple Cookies, 90
Greeting Card Cookies, 40

H

Half-Hearted Valentine Cookies, 46
Haystacks, 87
Heath® Bars, 80
Heavenly Almond Treats, 60
Hershey's® More Chips Chocolate
	Chip Cookies, 64
Hershey's® Vanilla Chip Chocolate
	Cookies, 63
Honey of a Cookie, 11

I

Ice Cream Cookies, 50
Irish Coffee Brownies, 30
Ivory Chip Strawberry Fudge
	Drops, 52

J

Jack O'Lantern Cookies, 43
Jam-Up Oatmeal Cookies, 14

L

Layered Fruit Bars, 76
Lemon Cookies, 20
Little Raisin Logs, 45

M

Magic Cookie Bars, 91
Maple Raisin Cookies, 23
Marvelous Macaroons, 6
Mint Frosting, 28
Molasses Applesauce Bars, 69
Mom's Best Oatmeal Cookies, 16

N

No-Bake Peanutty Chocolate
    Drops, 20

O

Oatmeal Apple Cookies, 22
Oatmeal Scotchies, 57
Orange Butter Cream Squares, 78
Oreo® Brownie Treats, 90
Original Toll House® Chocolate Chip
    Cookies, 60

P

P. B. Graham Snackers, 84
Peanut Blossoms, 12
Peanut Butter Bars, 77
Peanut Butter Chip Brownies, 32

Peanut Butter Chips and Jelly
    Bars, 88
Peanut Butter Jewels, 18
Peanut Butter Sunshine Cookies, 64
Pear Blondies, 83
Pineapple Almond Shortbread
    Bars, 68
Pudding Drop Cookies, 87
Pumpkin Cheesecake Bars, 83

Q

Quick No-Bake Brownies, 28

R

Reese's™ Cookies, 18
Refrigerator Cookies
    Almond Cream Cheese
        Cookies, 45
    Chocolate Refrigerator Cookies,
        6
    Ice Cream Cookies, 50
Rocky Road Brownies, 30
Rolled Cookies
    Austrian Tea Cookies, 48
    Buttery Jam Tarts, 88
    Chocolate Cut-Out Cookies, 51
    Greeting Card Cookies, 40
    Half-Hearted Valentine
        Cookies, 46
    Jam-Up Oatmeal Cookies, 14
    Raspberry-Filled Chocolate
        Ravioli, 42
    Walnut Cut-Out Cookies, 51

S

San Francisco Cookies, 54
Shaped Cookies
    Almond Fudge Cups, 48
    Choco-Dipped Peanut Butter
        Cookies, 12
    Chocolate Almond Snowballs, 12
    Chocolate Biscotti, 50
    Chocolate Cherry Cookies, 51
    Chocolate Chip Oatmeal Raisin
        Cookies, 62
    Chocolate-Dipped Brandy
        Snaps, 43
    Chocolate Oat Chewies, 9
    Chocolate Peanut Butter Chip
        Cookies, 57
    Chocolate Rum Balls, 46
    Cookie Pizza, 92
    Double Nut Chocolate Chip
        Cookies, 65
    Easy Peanut Butter Cookies, 12
    Easy Peanutty Snickerdoodles,
        59
    Fruit Burst Cookies, 22

Shaped Cookies (continued)

    Honey of a Cookie, 11
    Jack O'Lantern Cookies, 43
    Lemon Cookies, 20
    Little Raisin Logs, 45
    P. B. Graham Snackers, 84
    Peanut Blossoms, 12
    Peanut Butter Jewels, 18

    Spiced Molasses Cookies, 11
    Spritz, 23
    Whole Grain Chippers, 54
Spiced Molasses Cookies, 11
Spicy Pumpkin Cookies, 47
Spritz, 23
Strawberry Wonders, 75
Supreme Chocolate Saucepan
    Brownies, 39

T

Teddy Wants S'Mores, 91
Toffee-Bran Bars, 66
Toll House® Pan Cookies, 60
Tony's Tiger Bites™, 92
Tropical Orange Coconut Drops,
    15

U

Ultimate Brownies, 35
Ultimate Chocolate Chip
    Cookies, 62

W

Walnut Cut-Out Cookies, 51
White Chocolate Brownies, 26
Whole Grain Chippers, 54
Whole Wheat Oatmeal Cookies,
    8

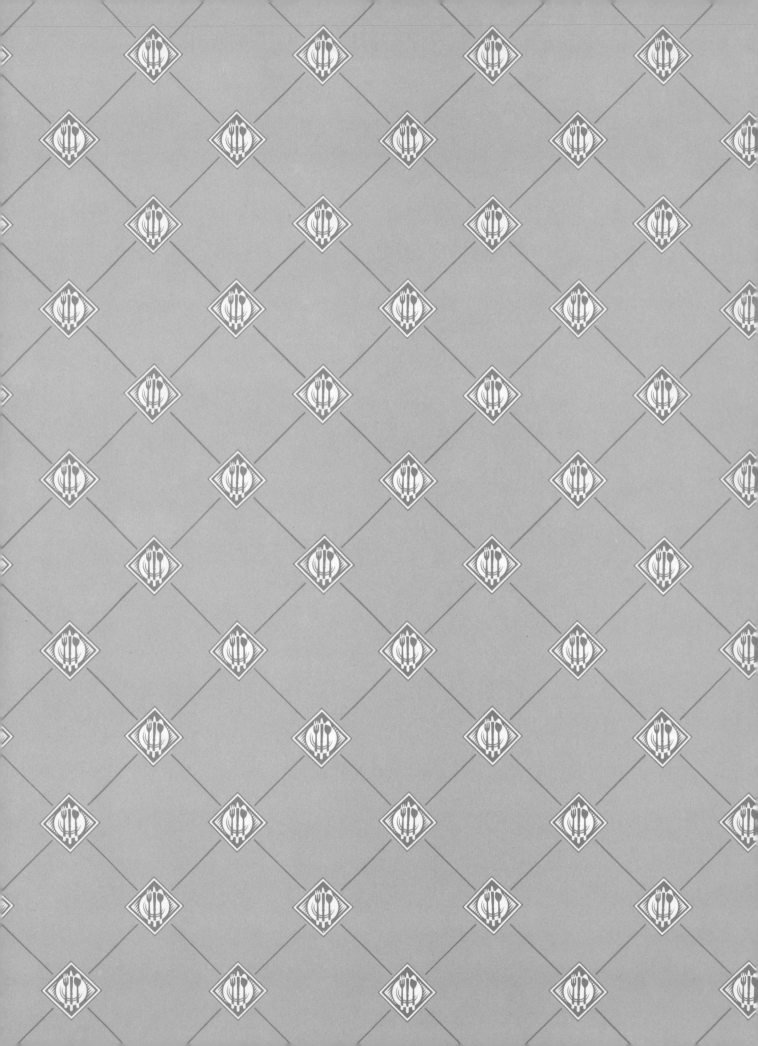